Geodesign

Case Studies in Regional and Urban Planning

by Shannon McElvaney

Table of Contents

Foreword

Technology enables a new relationship between humans and the environment. I've dedicated my life to building software to facilitate this enhanced relationship—a relationship where we are not just leveraging technology for business and military advantages but where we are actually using technology to design a better future and restore more naturalness to the world.

Man's first foray into changing his relationship with nature started when humans began to exploit earth's resources on a massive scale with little or no consideration for the environment. Over time, we started to understand the devastating effects of mass exploitation on our world—we reacted with conservation. Even with all the successes of conservation, it has proved to be an imperfect solution to restoring natural systems. But we humans are incredibly smart, and we have an amazing array of technologies available to extend our abilities. We may not be able to restore complete ecosystems, but we now have scientific and technical abilities to design them.

You and I are living in a world where we're going to have to move away from simply conserving places toward proactively creating healthy places. And this is what geodesign is all about: the consideration of comprehensive social and environmental information—geographic information—in the design process. Geodesign is about moving beyond just exploiting or conserving our geography and toward actually designing it; it's about the act of consciously designing a better future.

Geodesign represents the dawn of a new era in man's relationship with the environment: the age of designing. As we move from exploiting geography through conserving geography to the new paradigm of designing geography, we are redefining what it means to be masters of our environment.

As you read the case studies in this book, I'd like each of you to ask yourself a question: What is my role in designing a better world? And after you answer that question, ask the same question of your coworkers, your friends, your family, and people in your community. Because we're all in this together. I honestly believe that all of us, working together, with a little help from technology, have a very realistic chance of achieving our common goal: designing a better future.

Jack Dangermond
Redlands, California
March 2012

Acknowledgments

Bringing a book to life is much like writing and producing a song. You start with a seed of an idea, write the verses, a catchy chorus, the melody, and finally a bridge. But as soon as you start adding band members, their own talents, instruments, and voices change the mix and you end up creating something even better than you'd hoped for. And so this book was born.

Anyone who has played in a band knows that the drummer and the bassist form the foundation of the overall sound. They work together to give the music motion. In this case, Bill Miller provided the backbeat and got the project moving. His early work on geodesign inspired chapter 1, Game-Changing Design. Carl Steinitz played the stand-up bass, kindly providing me with well-tried case study guidelines and the geodesign framework with which I literally framed each chapter. To both I owe a debt of gratitude for private conversations, counsel, workshops, and presentations that helped me and many others form their early understanding of geodesign.

Of course, a good percussion section spices up a song just when you need it. Getting started and finishing a creative effort are definitely the hardest parts, but thanks to the folks at Esri Press, I was able to navigate the world of publishing and the daunting task of hunting down copyright permissions for all figures, photos, images, and text. I can't thank them enough, for both technical and moral support in the thick of things.

The rhythm guitars turned out to be a combination of skilled people at Esri Design Center and Office Services who helped design the cover, the layout of every chapter, and the proofing of text. The back and forth of countless edits and tweaks for days on end helped the book take shape. For all those who worked under tight schedules juggling numerous deadlines, I thank you.

And what band would be complete without a guest artist stepping in to add her talent. I'd like to thank Karen Richardson, Esri Marketing Communications, who helped me on chapter 6 (Building Smart from the Ground Up) by laying the groundwork with a shorter piece for Esri *ArcNews* on which I expanded to flesh out the geodesign theme for the book chapter.

Special thanks go to Matt Artz, who formed the entire string section and helped smooth out the rough edges and dissonance of the inevitable word jumbles. He is a true master with words and the language, and from him I learned a great deal.

Last, but not least, there are those who provided the content of the case studies and closing chapter. Their hard work and dedication to making the world a better place is obvious. Too many to mention here, but they are each included in the acknowledgments at the end of each chapter.

There is one additional person I'd like to thank, and that is my wife, Lisa McElvaney, with whom I talked many hours regarding various aspects of the book. She played an invaluable role as sounding board and adviser.

Game-Changing Design

Reframing an Old Idea

Design that considers or is influenced by its geography or landscape has been going on for thousands of years. The ancient Chinese were known to build settlements in close proximity to water with good mountain views to manifest their ideal of a harmonious landscape. The ancient Arabs designed their cities with narrow streets positioned to take advantage of the movement of the summer sun to maximize shading and the natural cooling effects of prevailing winds during the hot months. Issues of defense and proximity to trade routes and natural resources determined where a city was built. It made obvious sense to live near a spring, river, or forest rather than transport water or timber long distances.

Over time, technological advances, such as the steam engine, the train, the discovery of oil, and the development of the combustion engine, made it much easier to conquer and even defy nature. Bigger machinery made it possible to literally move mountains and extract resources at rates never seen before, with little consideration for the environment. The car, cheap fuel, and the building of highway systems led to increased mobility and the birth of suburbs. Industrial agriculture and the widespread use of chemical pesticides, herbicides, and fertilizers

Figure 1.1: For over 4,000 years, the ancient city of Fenghuang has exemplified the best in town site selection and layout, incorporating the artistic philosophy of Chinese garden design. (Image copyright Hung Chung Chih, 2011; used under license from Shutterstock.com)

Figure 1.2: The fortified town of Ait ben Haddou near Ouarzazate on the edge of the Sahara Desert in Morocco. Built on high ground for good protection, the earthen walls, as much as a meter thick, help keep the inside cool in summer and warm in winter. (Image copyright Seleznev Oleg, 2011; used under license from Shutterstock.com)

increased crop production. People became more prosperous, but it took its toll on the environment and public health.

Faith in industrialization, mechanization, consumerism, and mass construction paid little heed to biology creating an environment "ever more alien to life and its needs."[2] It was in this historical context that the influential architect Richard Neutra wrote *Survival Through Design* (1954).[3] Neutra was an early environmentalist, taking an approach to architectural design that applied elements of biological and behavioral science—what he called biorealism—or the "inherent and inseparable relationship between man and nature."[4] Design that values human

Figure 1.3: Incorporating plants and flowers into the building façade reduces heat gain and storm water runoff while cleaning air. (Image copyright Eugene Sergeev, 2011; used under license from Shutterstock.com)

physiology, psychology, and ecology—as opposed to always referring to the bottom line—was essential to human well-being and survivability. According to Neutra, "Community planning is an art, but one in need of a large scientific advisory board, chaired by an expert in biology."

Landscape architecture and planning were going through a similar evolution. In his book *Design with Nature* (1969), Ian McHarg advocated a framework for design that helps humans achieve synergy with nature.[5] In his view, design and planning that take into consideration both environmental and social values using the "rubric of chronology," or time,[6] help ensure the appropriate and responsible use of resources. McHarg's pioneering work using overlay analysis[7] had a

Figure 1.4: A typical suburb that really could be anywhere in the United States, an artifact of land use zoning practice that separates where people live from where they work. (Image copyright Tim Roberts Photography, 2011; used under license from Shutterstock.com.)

fundamental influence on the up-and-coming field of environmental planning and simultaneously solidified the core concepts of the young field of GIS.[8]

Both Neutra and McHarg decried design based solely on lowest-cost, economic drivers. But to move beyond a world where nature takes a back seat to low cost requires a shift in human values supported by sound government policies that reward nonpolluting, restorative business and commerce. According to Paul Hawken, renowned

"I believe that designing with nature, or geodesign, is our next evolutionary step..."

Jack Dangermond, Esri founder and president

"A prosperous commercial culture that is so intelligently designed and constructed that it mimics nature at every step, a symbiosis of company and customer, and ecology."

Paul Hawken, renowned environmentalist and author

environmentalist and author, it is possible to build a restorative economy based on "a prosperous commercial culture that is so intelligently designed and constructed that it mimics nature at every step, a symbiosis of company and customer, and ecology."[9]

Design also directly impacts public health. Heart disease, diabetes, obesity, asthma, depression, and traffic-related injury are now at epidemic proportions in the United States. A preponderance of research linking design and health led Richard J. Jackson, MD, MPH, University of California, Los Angeles, professor and author to state that the chronic diseases of the 21st century "can be moderated by how we design and build our human environment."[10]

During the 2010 TED Conference, Jack Dangermond took a philosophical approach to the question of design by comparing a Japanese garden to a suburb. The first—beautifully handcrafted by master gardeners to blend seamlessly with nature—took careful observation and deep thought to understand how each element affected the whole throughout the seasons. The second—a sprawling suburb of cookie-cutter homes carved out of a hill—stood in stark contrast as if "a crime against nature" had been committed. He proposed a "designing with nature" renaissance, publicly announcing geodesign as an alternative to traditional processes.[11]

These renowned visionaries and many more like them recognize the interconnectedness of humans and nature, the impact of the built environment on the health and well-being of both humans and nature, and the significant part that cultural values play in decision-making. The common theme here is that humans have unintentionally created many of the problems we face today and that we can ameliorate many of those problems through better design. But we can't do it alone or by using the same thinking that got us here in the first place.

Geodesign is a new way of framing an old idea, made possible by advances in science and information technology that were not available until recently. The variety and complexity of information and technology have grown, changing the dynamics of decision making. Issues that arise are complex, emotional, and often political, but it is our responsibility to come together in open dialog if we are to design a better world for future generations. And this requires a new way of thinking and a new way of working.

Figure 1.5: Dedicated bike lanes and ubiquitous mass transit help make bikes the main mode of travel in Amsterdam. (Image copyright Protasov A&N, 2011; used under license from Shutterstock.com)

"Simply put, design matters…designers have a critical role to play in the creation of a more just, healthful and sustainable world."

William McDonough, Twenty-First Century Design

Figure 1.6: The autumn colors in Ginkaku-ji, the "Temple of the Silver Pavilion" gardens in Kyoto, Japan. Harmony, serenity, and peace reign here. (Image copyright Paolo Gianti, 2011; used under license from Shutterstock.com)

Geodesign is a new way of framing an old idea, made possible by advances in science and information technology that were not available until recently.

"In a very real way, designers create the human environment; they make the things we use, the places we live and work, our modes of communication and mobility. Simply put, design matters. And at a moment in our history in which the scientific community has issued serious warnings about the negative impacts of our flawed designs—from global warming and water pollution to the loss of biodiversity and natural resources—designers have a critical role to play in the creation of a more just, healthful and sustainable world." William McDonough, Twenty-First Century Design[12]

Thinking Geodesign

Geographic information system technology, or GIS, has a complex pedigree. Born from landscape architecture, GIS and one of its close half siblings—design—have been intertwined, hard to separate, and competitive. Part of the reason has been that they are both holistic and interdisciplinary by nature, often only separated by job description or some arbitrary division based on real or perceived software limitations. GIS was seen as the place for mapping, planning, and analyses at the macro- and mesoscales, while CAD was seen as a design tool for engineering and architecture at the meso- and microscales. Those

5

> Geography is about place and processes, the human and the natural, across both space and time. It seeks to organize, understand, and describe the world.

> Design is about intent or purpose, the creation of something better, beautiful, or both—requiring rapid redesign and evaluation of design alternatives.

Figure 1.7: A shell, a spiral staircase, and the garden at Versailles. Some of the best designs are inspired by nature. (Images copyright Kuleczka, Gordon Galbraith, and Paul Prescott, 2011, respectively; used under license from Shutterstock.com)

boundaries, ill defined and arbitrary to begin with, are beginning to blur further with the introduction of geodesign. So exactly what is geodesign? Sometimes the best way to define something is to deconstruct it into its component parts, in this case geography and design:

Geography is about place and processes, the human and the natural, across both space and time. It seeks to organize, understand, and describe the world. "In a word, geography is a science—a thing not of mere names but of argument and reason, of cause and effect" (Hughes 1863).[13] GIS uses technology to organize, visualize, and analyze these physical phenomena, events, and processes to support problem solving and understanding.

Design differs in meaning among disciplines, but whether it is architectural or urban, interior or landscape, they all share common traits. Design starts with a need. It is about intent or purpose, the creation of something better, beautiful, or both. Design is a creative act requiring imagination. It can produce something entirely new or improve on something that already exists. It often requires the creation of a sketch or model, followed by a critique of form and function to determine whether it performs as planned. And finally, design is an iterative process, requiring the rapid redesign and evaluation of alternatives many times before the desired result is attained.

Geodesign combines the best of both of these worlds, providing a new way of thinking that integrates science and values into the design process by providing designers with robust tools that support rapid evaluation of design alternatives and the probable impacts of those designs. It provides the framework for exploring issues from an interdisciplinary point of view and resolving conflicts between alternative value sets. In this sense, it can be seen as an integral framework for intelligent, holistic design that "moves from designing around geography to actively designing with geography" (Artz 2011).[14]

A Deeper Dive

Imagine picking up a stylus and drawing a four-lane boulevard through a new area of town (figure 1.8). As you draw, a chart informs you of the cost of construction, maximum runoff, non-point source pollution loads, and the predicted number of vehicle-related deaths and injuries based on an assumed speed limit of 40 miles per hour. Additionally, air pollutants such as particulate matter, nitrogen, and sulfur oxides (i.e., NOx and SOx), and ozone, as well as greenhouse gas (GHG) emissions, are calculated as well as their impact on health and climate.

The number of injuries and GHGs are too high and need to be reduced. Shielding pedestrians from vehicles by graphically adding trees between the road and sidewalk, and calming traffic by adding curb extensions or "bulb-outs" to narrow the streets at intersections, lowers the predicted number of vehicle-related deaths and injuries, but not enough (figure 1.9). An additional enhancement is needed to meet your team's goals.

A decision is made to split opposing lanes with a median to further decrease vehicle-related death and injury. Someone then recommends changing the median type from concrete to a bioswale dotted with trees. The change reduces runoff, contaminants from runoff, and GHGs while saving lives (figure 1.10). The team is satisfied.

That is geodesign. It allows designers to do their creative design work while receiving near real-time feedback on the impact of that design, and do it with the same ease as pencil on paper. That is the vision or goal of geodesign: to provide a fundamental alternative to the way design is currently done. It can be a solitary act, but more often than not, it is a collaborative process of co-creation that facilitates innovation and the reaching of agreement on goals, leading toward better solutions, better designs, or a better future.

To understand this on a deeper level requires a greater understanding of the key characteristics of geodesign:

Geodesign is design in geographic space.

According to Bill Miller, director of GeoDesign Services at Esri, one of the most fundamental aspects of geodesign is that "design (the process

Figure 1.8: A four-lane boulevard. (Image by Esri)

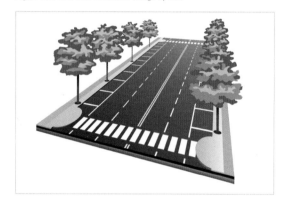

Figure 1.9: A four-lane boulevard with traffic calming features. (Image by Esri)

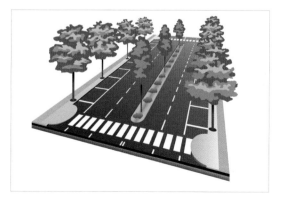

Figure 1.10: A four-lane boulevard with traffic calming feature and bioswale for a median. (Image by Esri)

Geodesign allows designers to do their creative design work while receiving near real-time feedback on the probable impacts of those designs.

One of the fundamental characteristics of geodesign is that "design (the process of creating or modifying some aspect of the natural or man-made environment) occurs within the context of geographic space"

Bill Miller, director of GeoDesign Services at Esri

of creating or modifying some aspect of the natural or man-made environment) occurs within the context of geographic space," that is, it is referenced to a geographic coordinate system.[15] That very simple act gives the designer the powerful evaluative power of GIS, the ability to quickly see and evaluate relationships and connections that would otherwise be missed.

Geodesign facilitates science-based design.[16]

This is nowhere more evident than in the ability to enhance design quality and efficiency by having ready access to information on geology, biology, ecology, hydrology, meteorology, and many other "ologies" during the design process itself. Building on McHarg's overlay analysis, GIS has extended its analytic capabilities to automate the calculation of hazards, risk, sensitivity, capacity, proximity, accessibility, and other analytics to inform design decisions. Most importantly, the impacts of those designs on the environment can be measured and weighed as part of the design.

Geodesign facilitates value-based design.

Creating design with respect to "hard" science, in many ways, is the easy part. The "soft" science of social values is actually harder to quantify and evaluate because it is often qualitative or based on personal views that arise from differences in culture, religion, class, education, politics, or age. From a design perspective, these can appear in the form of public policy (e.g., zoning, open space), ethics, and so forth. By designing in geographic space, the designer can get instant feedback on value-based content essential to successful design.

Geodesign provides a framework for exploring issues and resolving conflict.

Geodesign fosters collaborative decision making. As Tom Fisher, dean, College of Design, University of Minnesota, so poignantly stated, "GIS data mapping" and visualization enable us "to see the connections that our physical landscape and social structures keep separate and distinct."[17] Geodesign then brings these together so that participants from different backgrounds and different points of view can run what-if scenarios based on their assumptions and assess the consequences of those assumptions. More often than not, people are more in agreement than they realize, the discovery of which can make reconciling differences much easier to negotiate.

Geodesign improves the quality and efficiency of design.

Designing in geographic space improves the quality and efficiency of design. According to Michael Flaxman, Assistant Professor, Massachusetts Institute of Technology professor, "In an ideal case, a planner or designer receives real-time guidance on performance at every phase of the design from early site visit or conceptual sketch to final detail." The benefits to the designer of "improving designs-in-progress rather than on post-hoc evaluation"[18] are savings in design time and costs due to increased efficiencies such as rapid iteration, optimal use of constraints and opportunities, and better management of data throughout the design process.

Geodesign seeks to maximize benefits to society while minimizing both short- and long-term impacts on the natural environment.

"GIS data mapping" and visualization enable us "to see the connections that our physical landscape and social structures keep separate and distinct."

Tom Fisher, dean, College of Design, University of Minnesota

Figure 1.11: Droplets of rain adorn the web; a tear becomes a flood. (Image copyright Merlindo, 2011; used under license from Shutterstock.com)

Whether it's a building, a
city, a vast region, or the
globe, geodesign allows
designers to work on a
single design while taking
into account that design's
cumulative impact on the
whole.

Whether it's a building, a city, a vast region, or the globe, design in geographic space using a common reference system allows designers to work on a single design while taking into account that design's interconnectedness with other systems and its contribution to the cumulative impact on the whole. The water from a single drop is nothing, but taken cumulatively, they add up quickly. For a county the size of Los Angeles with nearly 10 million people, a half a gallon lost per flush of a non-dual flush toilet two times a day per person is 10 million gallons per day, or 3.65 billion gallons wasted in a year.

Geodesign is multidimensional.

Different design professionals require different design and visualization methods. A state trans- portation planner working on a new rail transit route may be most comfortable drafting potential routes in 2D, whereas the urban planner may need to view the impact of that rail through the downtown in 3D. The consultant hired to create the master plan may need to phase the develop- ment, adding time to the mix (4D). Any number of additional variables can be organized, evaluated, and visualized as necessary throughout the various design stages.

From Landscape to Geo-scape— Increasing Perspective

"What is your job on this project?" the contractor asked. "I'm in charge of everything that happens in space and time," joked the GIS manager. For a GIS manager on a large project, that can very well be true as he tracks and models all the moving

> "The geo-scape is the planet's life zone, including everything that lies below, on, and above the surface of the earth that supports life."
>
> Bill Miller, director of GeoDesign Services at Esri

pieces required to move a master plan forward through design phases and into construction. Managing when, what, and where something happens on the surface of the ground, under the ground, and in the atmosphere are all part and parcel of the GIS manager's job including structures, cranes, vegetation, and drainage on the ground; geology, utilities, subways, hydrothermal, and water tables below the ground; and impacts to air quality (dust, pollutants, exhaust), weather, sun movement, and airspace above the ground. The complexity and magnitude of the systems involved to design or adaptively manage a large-scale project require a broadening of perspective, from that of landscape to that of the *geo-scape*, defined as the planet's life zone.[19]

This life zone includes all regions of the planet that support life, including land and water, as well as everything below, on, and above the surface of the earth. This is the planet's life zone. It also includes the physical, biological, and social aspects of life, including our value systems and how we assess goodness, condition, and impact. Advances in information technology have made it possible to design and simulate the total impact of a design on the environment, and the environment on a design, before the design is ever built. Defining geo-scape as the planet's life zone gives us the ability to embrace and undertake much larger geo-based projects. It also gives us the ability to develop and maintain a balanced, multidisciplinary approach to identifying issues, resolving conflicts, and developing truly holistic solutions.

The Geodesign Framework

Carl Steinitz, professor emeritus in landscape architecture and planning at Harvard University Graduate School of Design, first described how the geodesign framework worked by posing it as a series of six questions relevant to landscape change.[20] The first three questions describe the world as it is and assess its condition (*assessment process*). The last three questions describe the world as it could be, evaluating proposed design alternatives and their impacts (*intervention process*).

The answer to the first question, "How should the geo-scape be described?" consists of abstracting geography into a series of inventory data layers. To answer the second question, "How does the geo-scape operate?" requires combining geospatial data using spatial analysis and modeling techniques to describe geographic processes and/or predict how spatial phenomena and processes might change over time. Answering the third question, "Is the geo-scape working well?" involves the creation of composite maps that combine a number of dissimilar things in a way that shows areas that are more favorable than others for certain activities. From Steinitz's point of view, the assessment process consists of examining existing conditions and determining whether the current conditions are operating well or not. Typically, the assessment phase involves the participation of a diverse set of subject matter experts and stakeholders who are involved in defining issues, metrics, and the proper method of analysis.

Once the assessment is complete, the geo-scape intervention process begins. Answering the fourth question, "How might the geo-scape be altered?" involves the sketching of design alternatives directly onto a geospatially referenced surface or data layer. The fifth question, "What differences might the changes

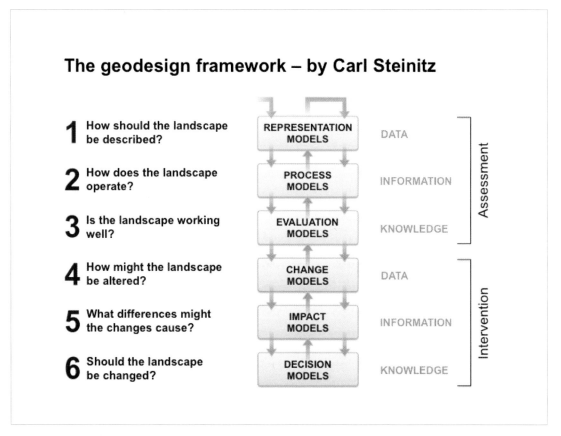

The geodesign framework – by Carl Steinitz

1 How should the landscape be described? → **REPRESENTATION MODELS** — DATA

2 How does the landscape operate? → **PROCESS MODELS** — INFORMATION

3 Is the landscape working well? → **EVALUATION MODELS** — KNOWLEDGE

⎫ Assessment

4 How might the landscape be altered? → **CHANGE MODELS** — DATA

5 What differences might the changes cause? → **IMPACT MODELS** — INFORMATION

6 Should the landscape be changed? → **DECISION MODELS** — KNOWLEDGE

⎫ Intervention

Figure 1.12: Carl Steinitz's framework, which uses a series of questions to guide the collaborating participants through the process of geodesign. (Courtesy of Carl Steinitz)

The geodesign framework delineates the conceptual framework for doing geodesign posed as a series of questions. The first three questions describe the world as it is and assess its condition (*assessment*). The last three questions describe the world as it could be, evaluating proposed design alternatives and their impacts (*intervention*).

cause?" is answered by the quick evaluation of the impacts of those changes. Finally, the answer to the sixth question, "Should the geo-scape be changed?" integrates considerations of policies and values into the decision process. The information produced by these impact models is used to help stakeholders and decision makers weigh the pros and cons of each decision factor so they can compare alternative solutions and, making the most informed decision possible, pick a preferred solution.

Geodesign in Practice

The geodesign framework provides an excellent conceptual diagram for proposing changes to the geo-scape over any scale. However, as the project grows in scale and complexity, so do the analyses. That is where the geodesign framework—empowered by integrative workflows, intuitive design tools, GIS-driven geoprocessing, and feedback dashboards—can really help guide a design project from start to finish.

The specific ingredients of each project will depend on the issues, participants, available data, information, knowledge, culture, values, geographic context, and available technology. The goal is that the geodesign framework will infuse design with a blend of "value and science-based information" made relevant by its geography and history to help designers and stakeholders make the wisest decisions possible, taking into account potential impacts.

To demonstrate the geodesign framework, several case studies have been chosen that exemplify key steps, processes, and/or technologies crucial to the advancement of geodesign. They are meant to be educational and illustrative of the burgeoning need for design that is able to simulate impact of design decisions in near real time, enabling decision makers to meet or exceed project goals, whether they be sustainability metrics, regulatory compliance, cost reduction, or faster response times in the face of disaster recovery. Given the convergence of technologies and advances in IT and cloud computing, it is likely that we will see the need for more of this type of design work, and geodesign can help.

Notes and References

[1] UNESCO World Heritage Convention. Fenghuang Ancient City web page. Retrieved August 1, 2011, from http://whc.unesco.org/en/tentativelists/5337/.

[2] Richard Neutra, *Survival Through Design* (New York: Oxford University Press, 1954), 26.

[3] Neutra, *Survival Through Design*.

[4] Juliet Farmer, "Richard Neutra's Biorealism Begets Green Design," ConcreteNetwork website. Retrieved August 2, 2011, from http://www.concretenetwork.com/concrete-architects/richard-neutra.html.

[5] Ian L. McHarg, *Design with Nature* (Garden City, NY: Doubleday/Natural History Press, 1969).

[6] Ian L. McHarg, Esri President's Award acceptance speech at the Esri International User Conference, 1997. Retrieved July 1, 2011, from video.esri.com/watch/127/video-of-ian-mcharg-at-the-esri-user-conference-in-1997.

[7] Prior to GIS, early overlay analysis was performed by physically mapping important design factors onto Mylar sheets. Each factor (water, species, land use, scenic, etc.) was drawn on its own transparency, darker gradations having the highest value and lightest gradations having the lowest value. When all the transparencies were superimposed by laying them on the original basemap, the darkest areas had the greatest overall value, and the lightest had the lowest. This technique laid the foundations for what would later become weighted multicriteria evaluation techniques common to GIS today to support evaluation and decision making.

[8] Jack Dangermond, "GIS: Designing Our Future," *ArcNews* 31, no. 2 (Summer 2009): 1, 6–7.

[9] Paul Hawken, *The Ecology of Commerce* (New York: HarperCollins Publishers, 1993), 15.

[10] Richard Joseph Jackson and Chris Kochtitzky, *Creating a Healthy Environment: The Impact of the Built Environment on Public Health*, Centers for Disease Control and Prevention Sprawl Watch Clearinghouse Monograph Series, Public Health and Land Use Monograph, 2010. Retrieved December 12, 2011, from http://www.cabq.gov/airquality/pdf/creatingahealthyenvironment.pdf.

[11] Jack Dangermond, *Jack Dangermond Talks about GeoDesign at TED 2010*. Retrieved July 1, 2011, from video.esri.com/watch/125/jack-dangermond-talks-about-geodesignat-ted2010.

[12] William McDonough, "Twenty-First Century Design." Retrieved May 13, 2011, from http://www.mcdonough.com/writings/21st.htm.

[13] William Hughes (1863), The Study of Geography. Lecture delivered at King's College, London, by Sir Marc Alexander. Quoted in J. N. L. Baker, *The History of Geography* (Oxford: Basil Blackwell, 1963), 66.

The goal is that the geodesign framework will infuse design with a blend of "value and science-based information" made relevant by its geography and history to help designers and stakeholders make the wisest decisions possible.

[14] Matt Artz, "Understanding Our World," *ArcNews* 33, no. 2 (Summer 2011). Retrieved August 1, 2011, from esri.com/news /arcnews/summer11articles/understanding-our-world.html.

[15] Bill Miller, in discussion with the author, March 28, 2011.

[16] Michael Goodchild, *Final Report* (June 10, 2001) of Workshop in Landscape Change, Santa Barbara, California, January 25–27, 2001. Retrieved March 16, 2012, from http://www.ncgia.ucsb.edu /landscape/final-report.pdf.

[17] Thomas Fisher, keynote address on geodesign, National States Geographic Information Council (NSGIC) Conference 2010.

[18] Michael Flaxman, Fundamentals of Geodesign (keynote address: May 22, 2009), *Peer Reviewed Proceedings of Digital Landscape Architecture 2010 at Anhalt University of Applied Science*, Buhmann/ Pietsch/Kretzler (eds.), (Berlin: Wichmann Verlag, 2010).

[19] William R. Miller, position paper on geospatial design. Specialist Meeting on Spatial Concepts in GIS and Design, National Center for Geographic Information and Science, Santa Barbara, California, December 15–16, 2008. Retrieved March 15, 2012, from http://www .ncgia.ucsb.edu/projects/scdg/docs/position/Miller-position -paper.pdf.

[20] Carl Steinitz, "A Framework for Theory Applicable to the Education of Landscape Architects (and other Environmental Design Professionals)," *Landscape Journal* 9, no. 2 (1990): 136–143.

2

Empowering the People

City of Asheville

Incorporated in 1791,[1] the City of Asheville, North Carolina, has grown from a small pioneering town into a flourishing metropolis known for its support of the arts and love of the outdoors. In 2010, *AmericanStyle Magazine* ranked Asheville #1 in its Top 25 Small Cities in America list,[2] and *Forbes* magazine ranked it #21 in its Best Places for Business & Careers list.[3] The arts thrive here with over 50 galleries representing every medium and more Art Deco buildings than any other city in the United States. Asheville also has six universities and colleges that contribute to the vibrancy of the city while producing an educated work force. As the largest city in western North Carolina, Asheville serves as the regional hub for business and has numerous community amenities such as theaters, parks, and open spaces for gatherings and events. Nestled in the Blue Ridge Mountains, Asheville enjoys a mild climate year-round, making it one of the Southeast's most popular destinations to live, work, and play.

Having a great place to live that is culturally and socially diverse is only part of the equation. Establishing a sustainable city requires creating a sufficient number of the right jobs that will keep and attract that all-important "creative class" of 25- to 35-year-olds to the city.[4] Despite the development over the past decade, city officials continue to actively seek investment, attract new businesses, and retain existing jobs and companies in the region. Among the city's number of programs that help support new businesses, investors, and government agencies interested in opening or relocating a business in

Figure 2.1: Left: Asheville in spring. Right: Grove Arcade, Center City Asheville. (Photos courtesy of the City of Asheville)

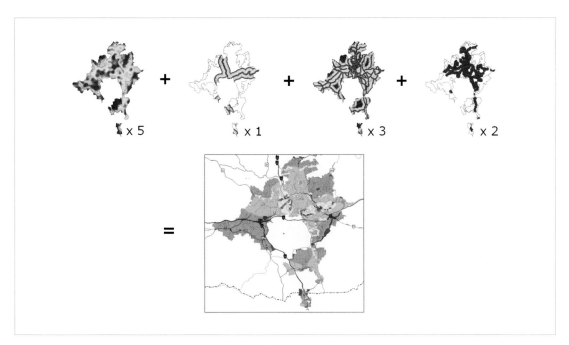

<x 5   + x 1   + x 3   + x 2

=

Figure 2.2: Weighted overlay analysis is a technique used for comparing the importance of dissimilar things using a common scale or set of values. In this case, certain factors like proximity to bikeways, bus stops, and rivers are more important than others, so before the factors are combined, the factors can be weighted based on their importance. The resultant composite map (often referred to as a heat map) shows areas that are more favorable than others using a red to yellow to blue color ramp. Areas of highest value are colored red, then orange, then yellow. Areas of lower value continue down the scale from cyan to light blue to dark blue, which signifies the lowest-value areas. (Courtesy of Azavea; data courtesy of City of Asheville and Buncombe County GIS)

Asheville is an interactive mapping program called Priority Places.

Location, Location, Location

According to the mapAsheville website, "Priority Places is a free, interactive mapping tool provided by the City of Asheville to strengthen strategic economic development and planning activities." The mapping tool facilitates business siting, neighborhood renewal and real estate development by enabling the identification of optimal locations for activities."[5] The website instructs users to select the criteria that matter most, weight each factor's importance, and create a "priority map" based on those choices as well as custom reports on a host of demographic data. It uses weighted map overlay analyses to create heat maps of sites that best meet chosen criteria (see figure 2.2). This is a form of site suitability analysis often used to answer the question, Where is the best location? For a commercial developer, it may be identifying locations for a new building that are in close proximity to a highway and then combining those results with land use (commercial, industrial) and population density. For a prospective home buyer, it might be identifying a home in an upper middle class neighborhood, near a school and shopping, with easy access to transit. The combinations are limitless. In fact, Priority Places can be used to plan any number of alternative scenarios to support planning and, ultimately, decision making.

"Priority Places is a free, interactive mapping tool provided by the City of Asheville to strengthen strategic economic development and planning activities."

City of Asheville, North Carolina

Decision factors can be selected and valued in any combination to provide truly customized site selections as many times as necessary to reflect any number of alternative scenarios.

Figure 2.3: Steps to create a prioritizing map: **Step 1**: Pick decision factors. **Step 2**: Indicate the importance of each decision factor. **Step 3**: Click the Create Priority Map button. Decision factors can be selected and valued in any combination to provide truly customized site selections as many times as necessary to reflect any number of different scenarios. (Courtesy of Azavea; data courtesy of City of Asheville and Buncombe County GIS)

Picking Places of Higher Priority

Imagine a business owner is looking for a new area to open a store, or perhaps she is thinking of relocating her company. Sustainability is an important company value, so she wants to consider green building strategies early on in the planning process as she seeks to maximize US Green Building Council Leadership in Energy and Environmental Design (LEED) certification credits.[6] To acquire credits, she wants to consider using existing building stock in close proximity to alternative forms of transit such as bike trails and bus stops. To lessen possible development fees, she would prefer an area with a high density of existing infrastructure such as water and sewer lines. Finally, she would like to look at areas that have a tax incentive for redevelopment. Additional info on crime rates, existing or planned development, and demographics would also help her with her decision.

The Priority Places process starts with the selection of a number of *decision factors* on which to create a priority map. Based on the scenario outlined above, she picks bike routes, transit stops, infrastructure, and tax incentives as her key decision factors. The next step is to score or weight each decision factor by moving the slider bar from the neutral (0) position to a preference value ranging from -5 (avoid proximity) to 5 (prefer

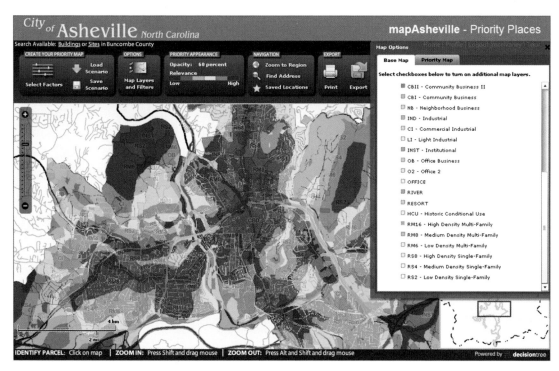

Figure 2.4: GIS is a great tool for reducing something that is computationally complex into an easily understood visualization. The heat map (shown here) provides an important data layer indicating the best areas to locate a new business overlaid with important zoning detail that can be used to help narrow the selection. (Courtesy of Azavea; data courtesy of City of Asheville and Buncombe County GIS)

GIS is a great tool for reducing something that is computationally complex into an easily understood visualization.

proximity). In this case, she increased the weights to infrastructure to 4 and low tax value areas to 5 (figure 2.3).

She is now ready and clicks the Create Priority Map button. The system runs the *assessment* models to produce a heat map highlighting the areas that best match the specified criteria (figure 2.4).

Additional features include "find an address" searches, customizable map color palettes, transparency controls, the ability to create bookmarks of specific map views, and the ability to save groups of decision factors and weights for reuse at a later date. Clicking directly on a parcel pulls up data regarding that parcel, such as the owner and parcel area, that can link directly to other

mapAsheville map services to show crime statistics or existing and planned development.

One of the most powerful elements of the Priority Places system is the ability to generate a number of demographic reports that provide information on the particular characteristics of a population in a specific neighborhood or area (figure 2.5).

Once a particular scenario is satisfactory, it can be saved and stored in a user profile for reimport and use later, printed as a map, or exported (as KML) for use in other applications or to share with colleagues.[7] Any number of alternative scenarios can be created.

Figure 2.5: Demographic reports can be created using a number of geospatial selection techniques. In this case, the Rings/Radii method was chosen, generating a search using overlapping rings at 1-, 3-, and 5-mile distances out from the selected parcel center point. This type of buffer analysis is a common geospatial query technique. (Courtesy of Azavea; data courtesy of City of Asheville and Buncombe County GIS)

Discussion

The Priority Places website was built by Azavea using its DecisionTree product, a customizable, high-performance geoprocessing and decision support tool. The application uses the ArcGIS® API for Flex, which incorporates the rich, interactive features made possible by the Adobe Flex toolkit (figure 2.6). Priority Places also utilizes the Esri Business Analyst Online℠ API, enabling users to produce an array of reports on demographic and economic characteristics, retail expenditures, and housing for areas surrounding their selected locations. It is relatively easy to use, has a free online tutorial, and requires no GIS knowledge or desktop software. As a result, Priority Places provides the general public with access to information and analysis that might otherwise be out of reach of many users.

From a geodesign perspective, Priority Places is a decision support tool that fulfills the *assessment* phase of Steinitz's geodesign process methodology. Although it doesn't support actual sketching of design alternatives, it does support the creation of alternative scenarios that are informed by their geographic context, both science- and value-based, providing an important function to the up-front preplanning often required by landscape architects and planners alike. It also supports the export of those analyses for use in ArcGIS or other

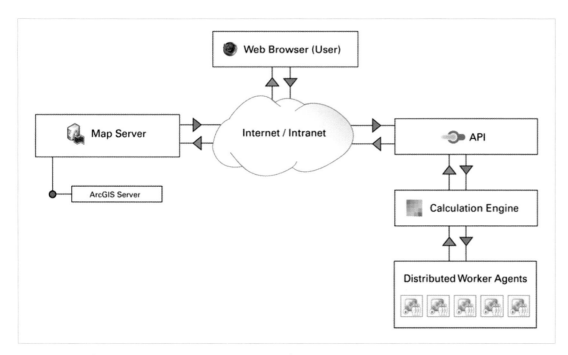

Figure 2.6: Diagram showing the DecisionTree system architecture. (Courtesy of Azavea)

Geodesign supports the creation of alternative scenarios that are informed by their geographic context, both science- and value-based, providing an important function to the up-front preplanning required by landscape architects and planners alike.

applications, key to many landscape architects' or designers' workflows.

It allows users to define important issues up front by the selection of decision factors, which will be used in the analyses. It utilizes a host of existing GIS data (*representation models*) that have already been compiled by the City of Asheville's GIS department into a common coordinate system and database structure.

The application allows the individual to weight the importance of each decision factor before running the models. This could be done by an individual or a representative of a stakeholder group for use in a larger planning effort. The DecisionTree software combines the user-defined weights with the decision factor layers to create assessment maps (figure 2.7).

Based on its calculations, DecisionTree then generates a hot spot or heat map displaying the locations that best match the selected decision factors and weights (*evaluation models*). Although Priority Places doesn't tread directly into Steinitz's geodesign *intervention* phase, it does utilize a good number of enabling technologies and geospatial processes worth serious examination for anyone venturing into geodesign application development.

Lessons Learned

The benefits of web-based spatial decision support are well known, having helped drive the growth of server-based GIS over the last 10 years.[9] The Priority Places map tool has capitalized on all these benefits and added a few:

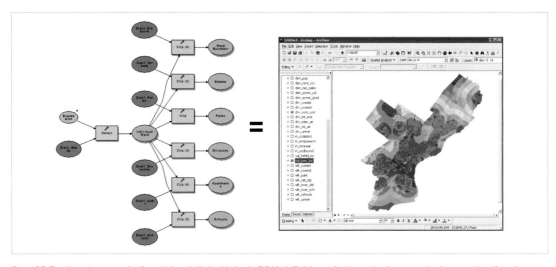

Figure 2.7: The above is an example of a spatial model built with the ArcGIS ModelBuilder application, a visual programming language that allows the user to build workflows that string sequences of events together, feeding the output of one tool into the input of the next. (Courtesy of Azavea)

Geodesign balances instant feedback with decision support tools to effectively and efficiently incorporate geographic information and stakeholder needs and preferences in the design process.

- Web-based spatial decision support tools result in significant economic savings.

- Centralizing models and decision support tools significantly simplifies the maintenance and distribution of such tools (version control, accessibility, storage).

- Data integrity is maintained through automated data verification routines.

- Models requiring intensive computation can be processed on servers or through a distributed network of servers in a fraction of the time they would take on less capable desktop computers.

- Web-based spatial decision support tools empower users, allowing them to identify site-specific options that meet their needs and perform analyses of alternative scenarios.

One of the key benefits of Priority Places is that it streamlines the evaluation of site suitability assessments through the use of weighted overlay analyses by never talking about it. Instead, individuals are led through the workflow with easy-to-use steps and an intuitive graphic user interface. The GIS modeling work is done behind the scenes, allowing the user to concentrate on the task at hand: finding the best place to build a business or home—or any venture for that matter.

A responsive user experience is important to a successful web application. Priority Places is fast. DecisionTree processes the models through a distributed calculation system that breaks up and distributes the work across multiple servers, and then reassembles the information in a fraction of the time it takes the same routine to run on a conventional server or standard desktop.[10]

As cloud computing and IT infrastructure continue to improve, it is likely that the same benefits that drove the adoption of server-based

GIS will drive the evolution of geodesign in the years ahead, only at a faster rate. People want simple. They want to click a button and get an answer. Balancing the need for instant feedback with sound decision support tools that effectively and efficiently incorporate a wide array of geographic data with consideration for user needs and preferences is fundamental to geodesign. For this reason and many above, Priority Places and the DecisionTree product on which it is built fill an important role in the continued evolution of geodesign enabling technology.

Key Links

City of Asheville, North Carolina
http://www.ashevillenc.gov/

City of Asheville, North Carolina, mapAsheville—Priority Places
http://gis.ashevillenc.gov/mapasheville/priorityplaces/

Azavea
http://www.azavea.com/

US Green Building Council
http://www.usgbc.org/

Acknowledgments

Thanks to Jason Mann, City of Asheville, and Robert Cheetham, Rachel Cheetham-Richard, and Tamara Manik-Perlman, Azavea.

Notes and References

[1] Old Buncombe County Genealogical Society, "A History of Asheville & Buncombe County," *The Historic News*, February 1999. Retrieved April 11, 2011, from http://www.obcgs.com/ashv_hist.htm.

[2] Jennifer Clary, "Top 25 Cities," *AmericanStyle Magazine* 72 (Summer 2010). Retrieved April 11, 2011, from http://www.americanstyle.com/2010/05/top-25-small-cities/.

[3] "Best Places for Jobs and Careers 2010: #21 Asheville NC," Forbes.com, April 14, 2010. Retrieved May 17, 2011, from http://www.forbes.com/lists/2010/1/business-places-10_Asheville-NC_2541.html.

[4] Richard Florida, "The Rise of the Creative Class," *Washington Monthly,* May 2002. Retrieved December 11, 2011, from http://www.washingtonmonthly.com/features/2001/0205.florida.html.

[5] City of Asheville, North Carolina, mapAsheville—Priority Places website. Retrieved April 2011, from http://gis.ashevillenc.gov/mapasheville/priorityplaces/.

[6] "What LEED Is," US Green Building Council LEED rating process web page. Retrieved May 17, 2011, from http://www.usgbc.org/DisplayPage.aspx?CMSPageID=1988.

[7] Josh Marcus, "DecisionTree Unveils a Redesigned Interface," *Avencia Journal* 4, issue 5 (December 2009). Retrieved January 31, 2011, from http://www.azavea.com/blogs/newsletter/v4i5/decisiontree-unveils-a-redesigned-interface/.

[8] "What is ModelBuilder?" Esri ArcGIS.com Help website. Retrieved May 17, 2011, from help.arcgis.com/en/arcgisdesktop/10.0/help/index.html#//002w00000001000000.htm.

[9] Shilpam Pandey, Jon Harbor, and Bernard Engel, *Internet-Based Geographic Information Systems and Decision Support Tools* (Park Ridge, IL: The Urban and Regional Information Systems Association, 2000), http://www.urisa.org/files/internet_based_gis_ebook.pdf.

[10] Megan Heckert and Robert Cheetham, "Bringing Multi-Criterion Siting Decisions to the Web," chap. 9 in *PhillydotMap: The Shape of Philadelphia*, Cartographic Modeling Lab, ed. (Philadelphia, PA: University of Pennsylvania, 2009). Retrieved January 31, 2011, from http://repository.upenn.edu/cml_papers/1/.

3

Fighting Climate Change

Place of History

Cape Cod has a rich and varied history, both cultural and natural. For centuries it has been the home of the Wampanoag tribe, the native people who helped the Pilgrims of 1620 survive their first winters. In fact, the Mayflower Pilgrims actually landed in what is now the site of Provincetown on the tip of Cape Cod before moving to Plymouth.[1] A few years earlier, Samuel de Champlain, Henry Hudson, and Captain John Smith had already charted, mapped, and noted Cape Cod as an ideal protected harborage for landing and settlement. By the time of Henry Thoreau's visits in the 1850s, the area had transformed into a well-developed fishing and whaling industry.[2] A hundred years later, Cape Cod had become a famous getaway of gray-shingled cottages for the elite. The Kennedy Compound in Hyannis Port, the Summer White House during John F. Kennedy's presidency, is one of the most well-known historic sites, having housed several generations of Kennedys. Today, the Cape, as it is called by locals, is widely known for its cranberries, oysters, lobsters, lighthouses, sailboats, and huge expanses of white beaches and natural beauty.

Figure 3.1: The Nauset Light, Eastham. (Photo courtesy of National Park Service)

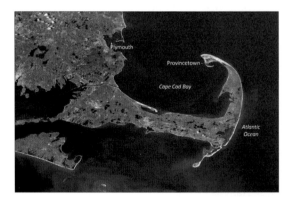

Figure 3.2: Fearing shallow waters, the Pilgrims dropped anchor just offshore of modern-day Provincetown, shown here in 2007 in a digital photograph from astronauts aboard the International Space Station.[3] Incidentally, this is where the Mayflower Compact was drafted and signed, binding together the voyagers into a "Body Politick," free of English law. (Image courtesy of Image Science and Analysis Laboratory, NASA-Johnson Space Center. "The Gateway to Astronaut Photography of Earth." Retrieved 4/1/2011, http://eol.jsc.nasa.gov/scripts/sseop/QuickView.pl?directory=ESC&ID=ISS016-E-10312.)

A Reason for Concern

It can be argued that climate change is a natural process. So is coastal erosion. But for some, like those who live on the Cape, this is of little comfort. The potential for sea-level rise and increases in storm intensity due to climate change, coupled with the impact of population growth and longer tourist seasons, have raised concerns among local and regional planning agencies about Cape Cod's future.

In 2009, the federal Interagency Working Group on Transportation, Land Use, and Climate Change, led by the Federal Highway Administration, selected Cape Cod, Massachusetts, as a pilot area to address climate change by facilitating and enhancing integrated regional and intermodal gateway mobility planning at the state, regional, and local levels. In 2010, the Volpe National Transportation Systems Center, a research branch of the US Department of Transportation's (USDOT) Research and Innovative Technology Administration, began work on the project. Funding support and overall guidance was provided by the Federal Highway Administration, National Park Service, and Fish and Wildlife Service, although other federal, state, regional, and local agencies played important roles. The goal was to take a systems or holistic approach to planning that looked across jurisdictional boundaries, assorted land uses, and transportation corridors in an attempt to understand their interconnected effects. In particular, the emphasis was on reducing greenhouse gas emissions from transportation and assessing the effects of climate change on land use and transportation infrastructure.

Cape Cod was the perfect place for such a proactive prototype project, a single geographic entity made up of 15 towns and numerous villages that would set aside differences and work together to protect the greater whole; an assemblage of issues on a microcosmic scale, the lessons from which could be applied to the macrocosm. Geodesign processes

Figure 3.3: Classic photo of fishing boats. (Photo courtesy of National Park Service)

and tools were well suited to this type of community-based strategic planning effort. A cornerstone of geodesign thinking is the linking of design or, in this case, proposed changes to the landscape, to relevant science-based information and value-based information, in a way that provides the framework for exploring planning issues from a collaborative, cross-disciplinary point of view.

The Volpe Center partnered with a multidisciplinary team that included PlaceMatters Inc., Placeways LLC, and the University of Colorado,

The goal was to take a systems or holistic approach to planning that looked across jurisdictional boundaries, assorted land uses, and transportation corridors in an attempt to understand their interconnected effects.

Geodesign provides a framework for exploring planning issues from a collaborative, cross-disciplinary point of view.

27

Geodesign is design in geographic space; that is, the design feature is referenced to a geographic coordinate system locating it in space.

Whether cultural or environmental, as soon as a feature is located on the earth, a wealth of interrelated information begins to take form through the organizational and analytic power of GIS.

Denver's Center for Sustainable Infrastructure Systems (CSIS) and the Transportation Research Center (TRC) to create and run a scenario planning workshop. From the beginning, the team planned to use Esri ArcGIS, Placeways CommunityViz, and TransCAD transportation modeling software. CommunityViz is an ArcGIS extension; that is, it extends the capabilities of ArcGIS in a unique way to facilitate local and regional planning through a variety of real-time analysis and visualization techniques.

Assembling and Assessing

The work began with the gathering and assembly of a reference geodatabase (figure 3.5) of diverse information about the area, including existing transportation infrastructure, land cover and land use, environmentally sensitive areas, vulnerable areas,[4] utilities, and transportation data from TransCAD (*representation models*). This data was all georeferenced, that is, it was tied to a specific place on the earth using a common coordinate system. Whether cultural or environmental, as soon as a feature is located on the earth, a wealth of interrelated information begins to take form through the organizational and analytic power of GIS. Suddenly, a local increase in land sales can be tied to the widening of a bridge 20 miles away, or a coastal algae bloom can be tied to nitrogen leaching from a number of septic tanks a mile upstream. By analyzing the spatial relationships and processes of both man-made and natural features, complex issues are easier to understand. It is these types of "issue" maps that serve as the background on which *evaluation models* can be built. *Evaluation models* typically depict the suitability, sensitivity, or capacity of the landscape to handle a particular land use (or set of land uses).

Figure 3.4: The natural environment is one of Cape Cod's most valuable assets. (Photos courtesy of National Park Service)

These *evaluation models* or their derivate maps are crucial to the geodesign process for they serve as the platform for developing alternative land-use plans (or land-use management strategies).

Where Do We Grow?

In addition to modeling present-day conditions, the team used population growth forecasts with existing land-use and transportation plans to create a number of *change models* (in geodesign parlance) to paint a portrait of what the Cape might look like 20 years in the future. How big would the population become? What type of land-use mix would be needed and where? How would this impact the environment? Alternative scenarios looked at combinations of development and transportation system improvements varying from extremely dispersed, with little change to transportation, to extremely compact, with planned and expanded transportation improvements. To conduct meaningful scenario planning for development and transportation options, growth assumptions had to be held constant for all scenarios:

- Growth horizon year 2030

- 28,000 net gain in number of households

- 63,000 net gain in population

- All growth in year-round population

- 15,500 net gain in number of jobs

The team used CommunityViz to develop these *change models* and prepare an array of indicators for measuring the range of impacts that each scenario would produce (figure 3.7). One

category of indicators explored the specifics of vehicle miles traveled (VMT) and GHGs; another focused on sea-level rise and other climate change impacts; and other categories enumerated preservation of natural/existing ecosystems, land-use constraints such as historic

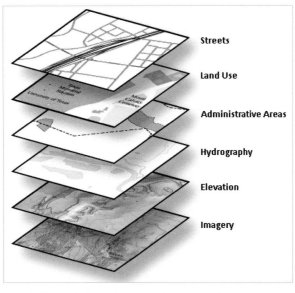

Figure 3.5: The geodatabase is the common data storage and management framework for ArcGIS. It combines "geo" (spatial data) with "database" (data repository) to create a central data repository for spatial data storage and management. (Image by Esri)

preservation districts and water resource areas, and transit accessibility indicators. Each kind of indicator used appropriate *impact models* derived from a range of scientific and empirical studies as well as more straightforward geospatial analyses.

One key model was a "5D" estimate of likely VMT reductions due to changes in residential and job *density*, neighborhood *design*, *diversity* of land uses, proximity to *destina-*

The team used population growth forecasts with existing land-use and transportation plans to create a number of *change models* (in geodesign parlance) to paint a portrait of what the Cape might look like 20 years in the future.

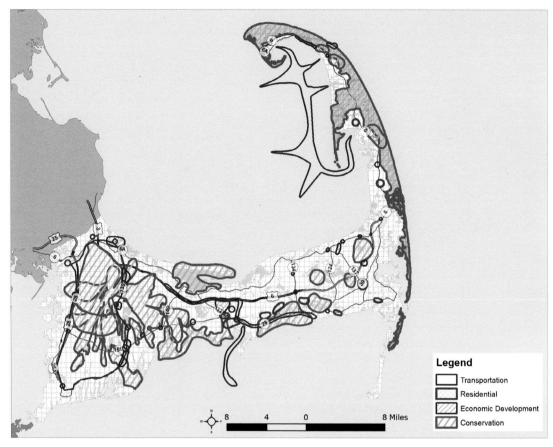

Figure 3.6: Part of data assembly involved the creation of a composite issues map using a combination of existing GIS layers and sketched additions gathered in the first day of workshops. (Figure courtesy of PlaceMatters and Placeways; data from Cape Cod Commission, MassDOT, MassGIS, USGS, US Census, and Volpe Center)

tions, and *distance* to transit. For example, if the diversity and density of land uses, jobs, and dwellings per acre are increased, the distance traveled per person decreases, thus lowering overall VMT for that community.

To give an example of the depth involved in a single model, let's explore the VMT reduction model. The essence of the 5D methodology lay in the "elasticities" used to adjust the vehicle trips (VT) and VMT forecast by traditional travel models. Travel behavior data is gathered either from household surveys or from conventional local traffic models. Regression analysis is then used to determine the effect that each of the five *D*s has on the number of vehicle trips and vehicle miles traveled while holding other factors, such as household size and income, constant. Ideally, different formulas are tried for each of the *D*s until the formula most appropriate for local circumstances, in terms of statistical significance,

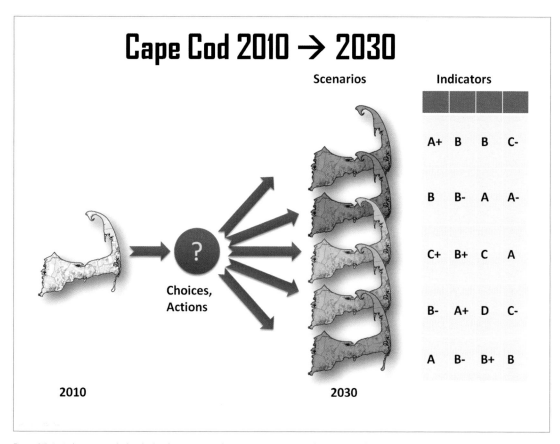

Cape Cod 2010 → 2030

Scenarios

Indicators

A+	B	B	C-
B	B-	A	A-
C+	B+	C	A
B-	A+	D	C-
A	B-	B+	B

2010

2030

Figure 3.7: An indicator is a calculated value that represents the impacts or outcomes of a scenario and its associated assumptions. For example, an indicator might be used to evaluate average household size, acres of habitat loss, total daily auto trips, or total transportation-related GHGs. (Figure courtesy of PlaceMatters and Placeways; data from MassDOT, MassGIS, and USGS)

is found.[5] In this project, the team used national averages as the starting point and then used CommunityViz features to make subsequent adjustments for local conditions.

In addition to the creation of indicators, a number of alternative scenarios were created in advance to support the workshops. These maps were designed to be intentionally extreme in order to point out potential pitfalls of design decisions and provide greater context for possible growth scenarios. These maps formed the jump-ing-off points from which workshop attendees could begin.

The major headings for these alternative scenario maps were *trend, dispersed,* and *targeted:*

Trend

- Each town growth at same rates as last 20 years

- No major change in transit programs

Key to the geodesign process is the ability to design in geographic space while receiving instant feedback about the impacts of design decisions.

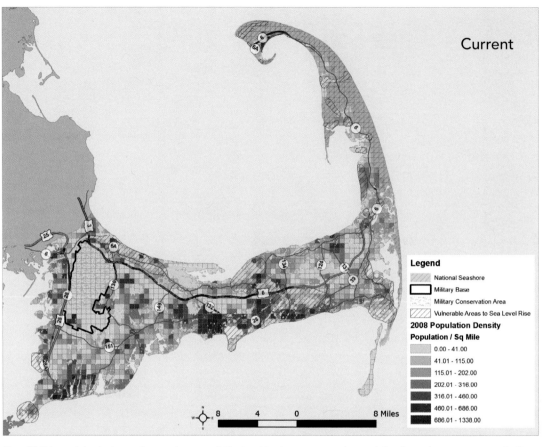

Current

Legend

- National Seashore
- Military Base
- Military Conservation Area
- Vulnerable Areas to Sea Level Rise

2008 Population Density
Population / Sq Mile

- 0.00 - 41.00
- 41.01 - 115.00
- 115.01 - 202.00
- 202.01 - 316.00
- 316.01 - 460.00
- 460.01 - 686.00
- 686.01 - 1338.00

8   4   0   8 Miles

Figure 3.8: This population density map illustrates the current distribution of development measured as population plus employment per square mile. The darker the red color, the higher the density. (Figure courtesy of PlaceMatters and Placeways; data from Cape Cod Commission, MassDOT, MassGIS, USGS, US Census, and Volpe Center)

Dispersed

- Development spread out

- Local growth proportional to local capacity

Targeted

- Development focused in key areas

- Near existing centers; in designated growth areas

- More planning judgment on case-by-case basis

Informed Design

Key to the geodesign process is the ability to design in geographic space while receiving instant feedback about the impacts of design decisions. Everything up to this point involved the collection of data and the creation of

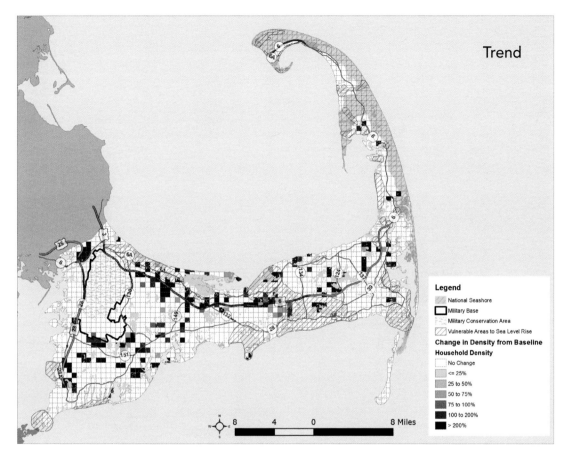

Figure 3.9: The population change in density map represents the trend of progressive growth over the next 20 years if the rate of growth remains the same as the last 20 years and if no major changes occur to transit; in this case, the darker the color, the greater the change. (Figure courtesy of PlaceMatters and Placeways; data from Cape Cod Commission, MassDOT, MassGIS, USGS, US Census, and Volpe Center)

Participatory planning tools like large-format tablets or the Wii-enabled infrared pen and touch table solution allow participants to sketch design ideas directly into the GIS.

process, *evaluation*, and *impact models* including key performance indicators by which the impacts of various design scenarios could be measured. Now it was time for local experts and stakeholders to convene for a hands-on workshop that began with short educational briefings on key community issues such as development options and trends; water quality; coastal erosion and sea-level rise; and the nexus between energy, emissions, and transportation.

Participants were then divided into small groups to work on these issues using interactive editing and sketching tools to explore potential variations to expected trends. The setup included a custom infrared pen system that allowed participants to "draw" on a projected image of the CommunityViz map and have their sketches entered directly into the computer (see figure 3.13). The Transit Alternatives exercise, for example, looked into possible extensions or

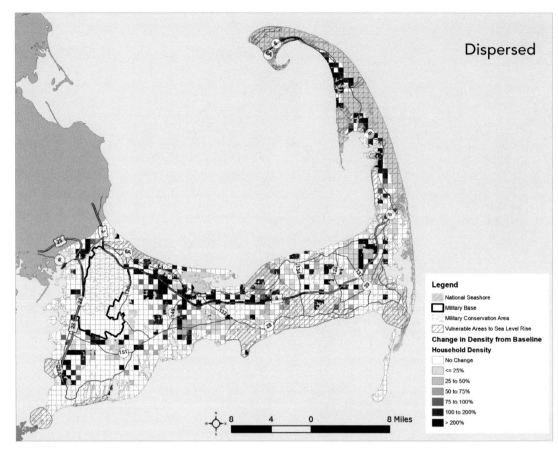

Figure 3.10: The population change in density map demonstrates what a dispersed pattern of growth might look like if development spreads out. This growth pattern is more conducive to continued sprawl, which typically includes the conversion of natural or agricultural areas to low-density, single-family land use. (Figure courtesy of PlaceMatters and Placeways; data from Cape Cod Commission, MassDOT, MassGIS, USGS, US Census, and Volpe Center)

changes to the planned transit routes in Cape Cod. After participants sketched new transit stops on the map, the CommunityViz impact model gave them dynamically updated information on important indicators like population served and GHG emissions. Based on the results, participants could choose to change their minds and revise their sketches.

Another exercise worked on deciding where to place new growth by placing virtual dots representing housing and jobs on the computer-ized maps. Again, the previously defined *impact models* provided stakeholders with instant feedback on important indicators for each iteration of a given scenario (see figure 3.14).

Discussion

The Cape Cod case study provided a real-life demonstration of key aspects of both the geodesign process and geodesign enabling technology:

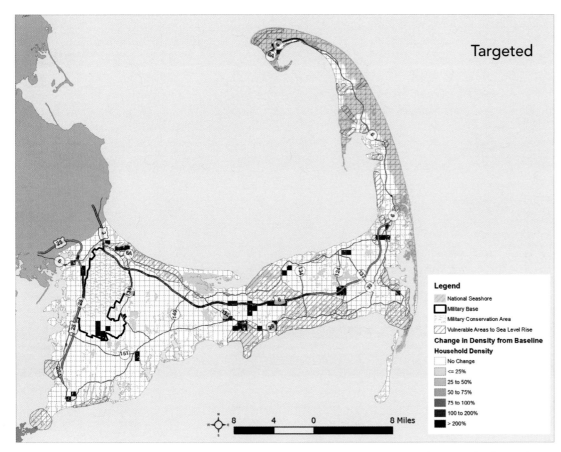

Targeted

This type of growth is much more in line with New Urbanism ideals typified by the creation of more compact, vibrant downtowns, which are argued to be more sustainable on a number of fronts.

Legend
- National Seashore
- Military Base
- Military Conservation Area
- Vulnerable Areas to Sea Level Rise

Change in Density from Baseline
Household Density
- No Change
- <= 25%
- 25 to 50%
- 50 to 75%
- 75 to 100%
- 100 to 200%
- > 200%

8   4   0   8 Miles

Figure 3.11: The final population change in density map shows what a targeted growth pattern might look like, one that focuses growth in designated areas near key centers. This type of growth is much more in line with New Urbanism⁶ ideals typified by the creation of more compact, vibrant downtowns, which are argued to be more sustainable on a number of fronts. (Figure courtesy of PlaceMatters and Placeways; data from Cape Cod Commission, MassDOT, MassGIS, USGS, US Census, and Volpe Center)

Sketching—A key geodesign enabling technology is the ability to rapidly sketch a design in geographic space. This particular example highlighted the use of an infrared pen on a large display, which entailed dragging icons (called "chips") representing particular physical or virtual objects (transit stops, numbers of housing units, or jobs) onto specific parts of the map (figure 3.13).

Spatially informed models—The modeling performed in this example made heavy use of georeferenced spatial information and calculations such as distances, densities, and networks. These are not functions that could have been performed using an ordinary relational database and help distinguish this case study as a good example of geodesign.

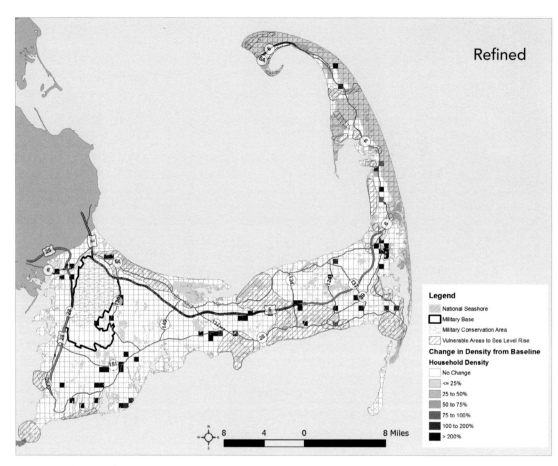

Figure 3.12: The final stage of the geodesign process—making a decision. The preliminary "refined" scenario map shown here represents a composite of transit, housing, and employment choices, one option chosen from a number of proposed alternatives. (Figure courtesy of PlaceMatters and Placeways; data from Cape Cod Commission, MassDOT, MassGIS, USGS, US Census, and Volpe Center)

Fast feedback—Technology improvements in the last several years have made it possible for exercises like this to work in real time, with participants seeing immediate indicator updates from their sketches. However, performance can still be a challenge. In addition to simply waiting for faster hardware, tool designers are taking two approaches to the problem:

- Performance tuning of geodesign models through mechanisms like selective indicator updates, precalculations, and algorithm tuning

- Moving more sophisticated capabilities to the cloud, or high-performance servers accessed via the web where tasks can be split up and completed on multiple servers in a fraction of the time it would take on a single desktop

Figure 3.13: The Wii-enabled infrared pen and touch table allowed participants to sketch directly into the GIS. With live GIS maps in front of them, participants could pan, zoom in and out, and view different data layers. (Photo courtesy of PlaceMatters and Placeways)

Iteration—The workshop was set up to allow participants to modify their sketches, immediately view impacts, and save multiple iterations during the design process. Additionally, the workshop encouraged design refinements through the merging of the small group results into a unified plan that took the best of each small group. However, due to the time constraints of the workshop itself, modification and merging of iterations were only minimally performed, and in most cases, sketches were refined further after the workshop.

Lessons Learned

In this example from Cape Cod, participants responded favorably to the digital approach to geodesign, saying the technology gave them new insights about factors they had not previously considered. The Volpe Center and its partners also learned some valuable positive and negative lessons about their specific techniques and about geodesign in general. These lessons correspond to similar anecdotal experiences in this and other

projects, which are good starting points for further research and discussion:

- The geodesign process is as important as geodesign technology. Both the benefits and the pitfalls of the process can affect outcomes as much as the tools themselves.

- Make sure there is enough time for participants to get used to the technology and perform iterations. If need be, make sure there are enough technology "drivers" (i.e., those who know the software and can drive the application) paired with facilitators.

- Local context is crucial, because design decisions make no sense without context. Because it is virtually impossible to predict what factors will be important in a local context, geodesign tools need to be flexible and easy to customize.

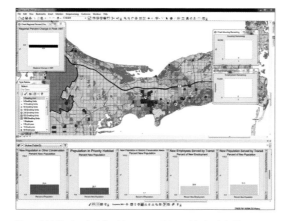

Figure 3.14: Previously defined *impact models* provided stakeholders with instant feedback on important indicators in the form of graphs (i.e., histograms) for each change made to the map. (Figure courtesy of PlaceMatters and Placeways; data from Cape Cod Commission, MassDOT, MassGIS, USGS, US Census, and Volpe Center)

One of the great advantages of geodesign is the capability to examine the effects of a proposed design across multiple interdependent systems.

Consistency across models and datasets is important yet difficult to achieve. One of the great advantages of geodesign is the capability to examine the effects of a proposed design across multiple interdependent systems (e.g., economic, environmental, natural, built). But if the models being used are inconsistent—for example, they use data from different years or they use different assumptions about external factors like population growth—their combination is not helpful.

Key Links

Placeways LLC
http://www.placeways.com/communityviz

Cape Cod Commission
http://www.capecodcommission.org

PlaceMatters
http://www.placematters.org

University of Colorado, Denver
http://www.ucdenver.edu

USDOT Volpe Center Pilot Project Website
www.volpe.dot.gov/coi/ppoa/publiclands/projects
/interagencypilotproject.html

Acknowledgments

Thanks to Ken Snyder and Jason Lally of PlaceMatters; Amy Anderson and Doug Walker, Placeways; and Dr. Bruce Janson, University of Colorado, Denver, Center for Sustainable Infrastructure Systems, for their contributions and the Volpe Center for its review.

Additional thanks go to the project's sponsors that include the Federal Highway Administration, National Park Service, and US Fish and Wildlife Service. Additional thanks go to many other federal, state, regional, and local entities involved in the project.

A number of case study details came from the Placeways Cape Cod case study PDF retrieved May 16, 2011, from http://placeways.com /communityviz/gallery/casestudies/pdf/CapeCod.pdf.

Additional information came from the PlaceMatters Lightning Talk given at the 2011 GeoDesign Summit (retrieved May 16, 2011, from video.esri.com/watch/86/2011-geodesign-summit-ken-snyder-cape -cod-scenario-planning-using-communityviz-and-diy-touch-table).

Notes and References

[1] Robert Arner, "Plymouth Rock Revisited: The Landing of the Pilgrim Fathers," *Journal of American Culture* 6, no. 4 (Winter 1983): 25–35.

[2] Henry David Thoreau (1865), *Cape Cod*, an annotated edition. Retrieved March 31, 2011, from http://thoreau.eserver.org /capecd00.html.

[3] "The Gateway to Astronaut Photography of Earth," Image Science and Analysis Laboratory, NASA-Johnson Space Center. Retrieved April 1, 2011, from http://eol.jsc.nasa.gov/scripts /sseop/QuickView.pl?directory=ESC&ID=ISS016-E-10312.

[4] The vulnerable areas layer was developed in July 2010 by a consensus-based expert elicitation, which involved local and regional coastal experts and drew on existing data and research literature. "Vulnerability" is based on elevation, erosion, and exposure to storm surge and sea-level rise.

[5] Association of Monterey Bay Area Governments (AMBAG), *Technical Report: Development and Application of the 5D Post-processing Tool* (December 2010), 6. Retrieved April 4, 2011, from http://www.ambag.org/programs/met_transp_plann /documents/AMBAG%205D%20report.pdf.

[6] "Density," New Urbanism web page. Retrieved April 8, 2011, from http://www.newurbanism.org/density.html.

4

Where the Wild Things Roam

The human history of the Yellowstone region goes back to an undesignated time in tribal oral history, more than 11,000 years ago[1] when many groups of Native Americans, including the Blackfeet, Apsáalooke (Crow), Shoshone, and the original Sheep-Eaters, used the park as their home, hunting ground, and source for gathering medicinal plants.[2] These traditional uses of Yellowstone lands continued until the first explorers and trappers of European descent found their way into the region, returning home recounting tales of a bountiful land full of natural wonders where "fire and brimstone" gushed up from the ground.

In March 1872, President Ulysses S. Grant signed into law a congressional act making Yellowstone the first national park in the world, an area so extraordinary that it was set aside and protected in perpetuity for the enjoyment of future generations.

Thanks to its early designation and protection, Yellowstone National Park is one of the few remaining intact large ecosystems in the northern temperate zone of the earth. Native flora is allowed to progress through natural succession with little direct management. The park's bison are the only wild, continuously free-ranging bison remaining of

Figure 4.1: A winter morning on the prairie. (Photo courtesy of Hamilton Greenwood)

the vast herds that once covered the plains,[3] and in 1995 and 1996, gray wolves were reintroduced to the wild here, reestablishing an important predator-prey balance to the ecosystem.

In recent years, managing these resources has become increasingly challenging. Drought, wildfire, habitat fragmentation, contaminants, invasive species, disease, and a rapidly changing climate have begun to threaten human populations as well as native species and their habitats. To plan for this uncertainty, a dedicated group of ecologists are using ArcGIS, statistical analyses, and a geodesign workflow to measure the impact of potential land-use change before it happens.

Ecological Forecasting

The Yellowstone Ecological Research Center (YERC), a private, nonprofit organization located in Montana, spends much of its time conducting long-term, large-scale, collaborative ecological research and education in concert with both public and private organizations.[4] Historically, that work has relied heavily on ArcGIS to help organize, analyze, and visualize data on the health and status of native species and the land and water on which they survive. But what happens to protected species if annual temperatures increase by 2 degrees Fahrenheit? What happens to a species if a new road is built through a prime feeding ground?

To answer these questions, legacy environmental and species data can be used to identify historic population trends in the hopes of projecting or predicting future outcomes. It is not possible to predict the future with certainty, but you can plan ahead for probable events. If the weather station forecasts an 80 percent chance of rain tomorrow, most people grab an umbrella or

Figure 4.2: The prairie supports bison, pronghorn antelope, coyote, and an assortment of other creatures. (Photos courtesy of Hamilton Greenwood)

change their plans. Following that analogy, YERC ecologists use the term *ecological forecasting* to represent the method they use to plan for any number of alternative what-if scenarios that might adversely impact the landscape or habitat of a protected species.

Simulating ecological system dynamics is a complex undertaking. The sheer volume, variety, and complexity of geospatial data has grown exponentially in recent years, requiring the

YERC ecologists use the term *ecological forecasting* to represent the method they use to plan for any number of alternative what-if scenarios that might adversely impact the landscape or habitat of a protected species.

Geodesign, in essence, is a decision support methodology that closely couples design activities with near real-time impact simulations informed by geographic knowledge — information on the physical aspects of the environment and human values.

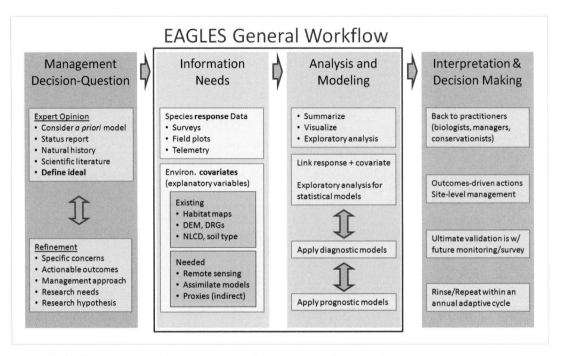

EAGLES General Workflow

Management Decision-Question	Information Needs	Analysis and Modeling	Interpretation & Decision Making
Expert Opinion • Consider *a priori* model • Status report • Natural history • Scientific literature • **Define ideal**	Species **response** Data • Surveys • Field plots • Telemetry	• Summarize • Visualize • Exploratory analysis	Back to practitioners (biologists, managers, conservationists)
	Environ. **covariates** (explanatory variables)	Link response + covariate Exploratory analysis for statistical models	Outcomes-driven actions Site-level management
	Existing • Habitat maps • DEM, DRGs • NLCD, soil type	Apply diagnostic models	Ultimate validation is w/ future monitoring/survey
Refinement • Specific concerns • Actionable outcomes • Management approach • Research needs • Research hypothesis	Needed • Remote sensing • Assimilate models • Proxies (indirect)	Apply prognostic models	Rinse/Repeat within an annual adaptive cycle

Figure 4.3: The EAGLES workflow schematic diagram. (Courtesy of the Yellowstone Ecological Resource Center)

development of new tools and efficient workflows to help decision makers spend more time on the issues, not sorting through data. More importantly, decision makers need to be able to synthesize this data into *standardized*, *transparent*, and *defensible* information to support the management needs of today while preparing for the needs of tomorrow. And that means having a *repeatable* process, a core tenet of scientific inquiry.

To support the entire process of ecological forecasting, YERC ecologists, statisticians, and GIS analysts created the Ecosystem Assessment, Geospatial Analysis and Landscape Evaluation System, known as EAGLES. EAGLES is an integrative workflow architecture that organizes vast amounts of historic spatial data, some covering the entire United States, with modeling routines to create predictive ecosystem and species models. ArcGIS is a key component of EAGLES, providing a mapping platform to make the data easily understandable to decision makers.

EAGLES—Geodesign at an Ecosystem Scale

EAGLES is essentially geodesign at an ecosystem scale. Geodesign, in essence, is a decision support methodology that closely couples design activities with near real-time impact simulations informed by geographic knowledge—information on the physical aspects of the environment and human values. In this case, design has more to do with adaptive management planning in response to possible land-use changes due to natural events,

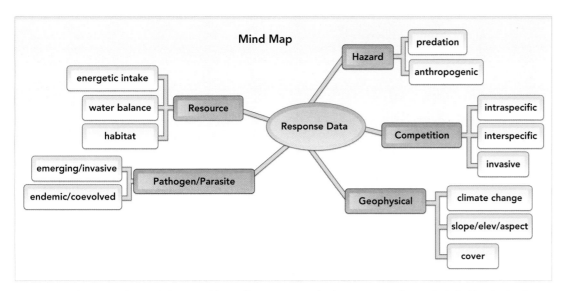

Figure 4.4: A mind map is a quick way to display potential factors affecting variation in a focal species response, for example, the health and vitality of a population. The mind map could be based on present-day data or legacy datasets, either of which helps visualize the narrative model, which can get rather complex.[5] The narrative model will eventually be used to create a quantitative model to support statistical analytics that occur later in the workflow. (Courtesy of the Yellowstone Ecological Resource Center)

although it can also be applied to local man-made events like the building of a new road or some other development.

The EAGLES workflow closely parallels Steinitz's geodesign framework using a workflow that guides practitioners through both assessment and intervention models. ArcGIS for Desktop tools and web-enabled environments provide a systematic yet flexible architecture for the integration of species data with environmental data to assess condition, create model parameters, and simulate impact of various scenarios. As each model is run, it is tested statistically against real data until the models "fit" reality well enough that they can be used to forecast probable future impacts.

The following is a breakdown of how a typical project might proceed through the EAGLES workflow.

Define the Management Decision or Question to Be Investigated

The workflow begins with the assembly of experts with a strong knowledge of the organism of interest, including physiological drivers, feeding habits, predator-prey relationships, competitive interactions, and habitat. Additionally, this effort can integrate pathogens, parasites, or other hazards. These experts help develop a conceptual model of key issues and management objectives. The conceptual modeling process begins with a verbal description of important relationships between the species of interest and its environment. The verbal description is then used to help select a set of hypothetical drivers to be considered for inclusion in the model. Here, we refer to the environmental variables (i.e., covariates) and their relationship to the species of interest (i.e., response data) as a narrative model using a mind map (figure 4.4).

ArcGIS for Desktop tools and web-enabled environments provide a systematic yet flexible architecture for the integration of species data with environmental data to assess condition, create model parameters, and simulate impact of various scenarios.

Figure 4.5: Pronghorn antelope. (Photo courtesy of Hamilton Greenwood)

This study, led by P.J. White, YNP, focused on the following:

- Demographic monitoring, especially recruitment and survival

- Ecological interactions, especially predation rates and recruitment

- Habitat assessment

The issue assessment resulted in the creation of two narrative models, one representing *birthing arenas* and another for *resource selection* (involving the identification and use of viable habitats). In this case, species vitality could be explained by forage availability, predator intensity, geophysical context, and climatic variables; for example, the more rain, the more food, the more newborns, the healthier the population might become.

Information Needs

Once the narrative models have been created, the next step is the identification and gathering of relevant datasets (*representation models*) to support the development of numerous *process* and *evaluation models*. Data inputs can be classified into two broad groups: (1) spatially explicit and/or time series species observation data (i.e., response data), including locations, sightings, nest sites, GPS, telemetry data, sign, mortality sites, survey and transect data, and (2) environmental geospatial data (i.e., explanatory data). Environmental geospatial data can be static variables such as slope, aspect, elevation, existing habitat, and vegetation cover, or it can be dynamic variables that vary over time such as climatic metrics (such as minimum or maximum temperature, fire intensity, flooding, percent surface water, and forage biomass).

Considering all possible risks and rewards based on expert opinion, research, and natural history helps avoid making inadequate models. Ideally, the mind map model and subsequent quantitative models represent factors that may affect populations, in the context of postulated mechanisms leading to testable hypotheses and management decisions.

For example, the Yellowstone National Park (YNP) pronghorn antelope (*Antilocapra americana*) faces a suite of risks characteristic of small populations with geographic/demographic isolation, low abundance, and low recruitment. Decision makers need a management plan based on demographic monitoring of abundance, especially species vitality rates.

The following environmental geospatial data was needed to answer questions regarding road, predator, and range condition impacts on pronghorn antelope:

Abiotic

- Elevation
- Slope
- Topographic complexity

Biotic: Productivity

- Forage
- Net primary production (NPP)[6]

Biotic: Land cover

- Percent forest cover
- Percent sagebrush cover
- Percent herbaceous cover
- Percent soil cover

Biotic: Predation

- Coyote intensity of use
- Wolf intensity of use
- Small mammal (prey) prevalence

Human Influenced

- Distance to roads

One of the big advantages of EAGLES is the ease with which relevant geospatial data can be found, processed, and made ready for use in ArcGIS. A wiki provides an index of existing geospatial data, as well as information on its content and generation,[7] and COASTER (Customized Online Aggregation & Summarization Tool for Environmental Rasters)[8] allows anyone to customize climatic variables for a particular area, period of time, and spatial resolution and download them for immediate use with ArcGIS (figure 4.7). The climatic data comes from National

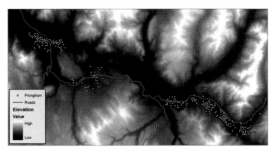

Figure 4.6: Environmental maps representing (a) elevation, (b) forage, and (c) percent sage cover overlaid with pronghorn locations shown as yellow dots and roads as red lines. (Figures courtesy of the Yellowstone Ecological Resource Center; data courtesy of YERC, NPS, USGS, ArcUSA, and Esri)

Aeronautics and Space Administration (NASA) and spans over 30 years, with more data added daily.

Data Integration

Preparing GIS data for use on any project can be time-consuming and frustrating. EAGLES simplifies the integration of species data with environmental datasets by using the Resource Selection

One of the big advantages of EAGLES is the ease with which relevant geospatial data can be found, processed, and made ready for use in ArcGIS.

COASTER (Customized Online Aggregation & Summarization Tool for Environmental Rasters) allows anyone to customize climatic variables for a particular area, period of time, and spatial resolution and download them for immediate use with ArcGIS.

Once the data is prepared, describing the landscape and defining how it operates, the evaluative modeling can occur (*evaluation models*) to determine whether the landscape is working well.

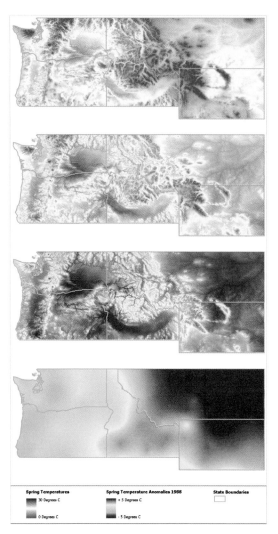

Spring Temperatures

30 Degrees C

0 Degrees C

Spring Temperature Anomalies 1988

+ 5 Degrees C

- 5 Degrees C

State Boundaries

Figure 4.7: COASTER was used to produce an assessment of spring temperature anomalies for five western states (bounded by green line work). A blue-yellow-orange-red color ramp displays variation from -5C to +5C, signifying cooler to warmer temperature changes. (Figure courtesy of the Yellowstone Ecological Resource Center; data courtesy of YERC, USGS, NASA Ames Research Center, ArcUSA, US Census, and Esri)

Probability Function (RSPF). The tool, based on ArcGIS, helps organize and resample data to user-defined grid resolutions and supports the creation of merged data arrays (MDA)—basically a table created from the intersection of all environmental values by spatial location—great for use in statistical programming environments. The RSPF tool combines a number of tedious steps involved in preparing data for export, greatly streamlining an otherwise time-consuming process.

In the case of the pronghorn antelope study, the species observations included 762 telemetry fixes from 26 collared animals from May to July of 2005 (visible as the top layer of the data integration stack in figure 4.8). The *spatial extent* of analysis was defined by this data in combination with expert knowledge of known habitat use. The *spatial resolution* for all environmental data was a 100-meter grid produced by resampling of the data as appropriate.

Various modeling techniques were used to create forage, herbaceous, sage, soil, and cumulative NPP layers (*process models*). Additional models using empirical field data created coyote and wolf intensity of use and small mammal biomass layers. Finally, *available space* layers were created using one-kilometer buffers around each pronghorn location in which points were randomly generated over that space to simulate potential habitat use. Since the spatial scale at which pronghorn select their habitat was unknown, this process was repeated at three kilometers and five kilometers for comparative analysis.

Analysis and Modeling

Once the data is prepared, describing the landscape and defining how it operates, the evaluative modeling can occur (*evaluation models*) to determine whether the landscape is working well. This involves a number of statistical analyses that occur in the open source statistical programming environment R, which is accessed from within the

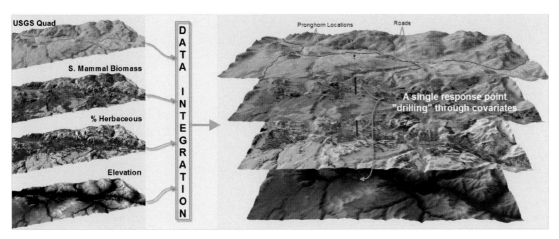

Figure 4.8: When all data is referenced to a common coordinate system, the referential link gives the scientist or manager the ability to investigate all the various interdependencies of a single point to all other data, increasing the efficiency and quality of inquiry. (Figure courtesy of the Yellowstone Ecological Resource Center; data courtesy of YERC, NPS, USGS, ArcUSA, and Esri)

ArcGIS environment. EAGLES uses the RSPF tool to create species distribution models and a statistical model for intensity of use. Optimization routines (e.g., Nelder-Mead, simulated annealing) are used to "fit" the model to the available data and associated assumptions (figure 4.9).

Model Assessment and Interpretation

Results from the preliminary data exploration and analysis both require a degree of statistical understanding to effectively build a model and interpret the results. For a model to be scientifically defensible, it should meet two criteria: (1) it should be the best model of a suite of candidate models, and (2) it should provide an adequate overall fit to the data.

The EAGLES tools provide users with a number of statistical mechanisms for addressing these criteria. The intent of EAGLES is to provide users with access to a powerful modeling and visualization framework without requiring extensive statistical programming knowledge.

Examining Alternative Futures— Ecological Forecasting

EAGLES has a tool called the Swap tool that enables users to build alternative scenarios (*change models*) using an already constructed model and change only one attribute while holding all else constant to examine the effects of that change on the model. This approach allows a transparent investigation of the changes in levels of treatments such as geophysical layer alterations, changes in forage availability, or more sophisticated modeled input layer substitutions. The goal is to apply a model previously fit to observed data to a potential scenario, in an effort to make projections about the ecological ramifications of a given landscape change (*impact models*).

For example, a forecast about the impact of building a new road through a habitat would rely on the input of a new layer that contains the proposed road (figure 4.10). The user can then apply the fitted RSPF model to the new road

The goal is to apply a model previously fit to observed data to a potential scenario, in an effort to make projections about the ecological ramifications of a given landscape change (*impact models*).

49

Geodesign starts by defining key issues of concern that frame the question or hypothesis to be considered to meet management objectives.

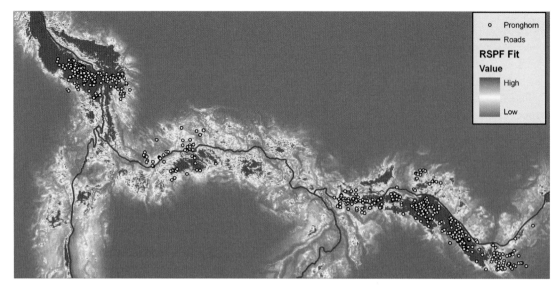

Figure 4.9: The final component of the RSPF output is the predicted RSPF surface for the best model, which is fitted and displayed in ArcGIS. Again, pronghorn observations are represented by yellow dots and roads as red lines. Percent of species/habitat model fit from high to low is represented by a color ramp that goes from brown to yellow to blue, with brown being a good fit and blue being a low fit. The prediction for pronghorn habitat use looks reasonable based on biological knowledge of this system: the large swatch of good habitat that is apparently not used in the upper left-hand corner of the surface is a traditional winter range. (Figure courtesy of the Yellowstone Ecological Resource Center; data courtesy of YERC, NPS, USGS, ArcUSA, and Esri)

layer (instead of the original layer) and view the response surface under the changed landscape. Such projections allow a measured assessment of habitat change. Visualization of the resulting surface occurs in GIS, and the resulting equations and models can be examined statistically as well. The intent is to provide a utility for planning for landscape change.

The Swap tool resides within the RSPF functionality and can be applied to an RSPF model and surface once a hypothesized alteration to the landscape has been built. Additional types of alternate landscape conditions include products such as expected forest density after thinning, forage production after burning, or NPP change under a future climate scenario.

Discussion

The EAGLES workflow closely parallels the geodesign workflow fulfilling both the *assessment* and *intervention* phases of Steinitz's model. It starts by defining key issues of concern that *frame* the question or hypothesis to be considered to meet management objectives. This in turn identifies the data needs and drives data collection and integration using customized search and data integration techniques that streamline the compilation of species and environmental geospatial datasets. This data (*representation models*) forms the backbone of the *assessment* phase.

In addition, EAGLES includes a number of procedures for the creation of *process models* that describe both static and temporal aspects of ecosystem processes. Elevation, slope, soil, wetness, productivity, forage, and vegetation cover are all derived from a multitude of datasets that represent the physical processes of the environment. These, as well as other datasets and tools like COASTER, are used to create assessment models that evaluate the condition or suitability of the environment, particularly with respect to capacity, hazards, or resources for a given species (*evaluation models*).

EAGLES is designed to aid resource management decision making by providing support for species habitat planning efforts that integrate changing landscape conditions with demographic responses. Managers seeking to evaluate multiple development plan proposals can use this system to compare alternative scenarios (*change models*), including changes in land-use practices, and explore their impli-cations using hypothetical what-if scenarios (*impact models*). For example, managers can use this set of tools to investigate how a species of concern currently uses a portion of landscape and how that use pattern might change when

the landscape is altered (e.g., through fire, flood, or development).

Lessons Learned

One of the obstacles to rapid adoption of the geodesign concept by the design disciplines is the time it takes to find, compile, and integrate relevant data into a common format for use in analyses. A second stumbling block occurs in the difficulty of tracking, archiving, and making available the complex data inputs that feed into ecological and species modeling efforts. One benefit of the EAGLES toolset is that it actually streamlines this process by allowing users to identify the geospatial data inputs, the region of interest, the scale, a common data resolution, and even a temporal resolution to make it easier to assemble available national datasets into a common georeferenced coordinate system using ArcGIS. Applying such a workflow to standardized datasets across the United States would help propel the adoption of geodesign.

Managers seeking to evaluate multiple development plan proposals can use this system to compare alternative scenarios, including changes in land-use practices, and explore their implications using hypothetical what-if scenarios.

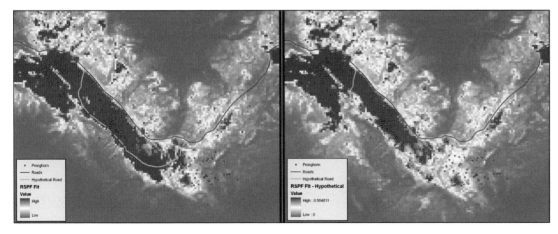

Figure 4.10: The map on the left displays a portion of the original RSPF model showing predicted habitat use for pronghorn in Yellowstone National Park. The Swap tool was used to apply the RSPF model to a hypothetical road addition (shown in green). The new prognostic RSPF model output for pronghorn (right) indicates that pronghorn would be excluded from portions of their original selected habitats. (Figures courtesy of the Yellowstone Ecological Resource Center; data courtesy of YERC, NPS, USGS, ArcUSA, US Census, and Esri)

When changes to the landscape are proposed, or seen as inevitable, in the case of natural disturbances or climate change, alternative scenarios can be considered and plans put in place to minimize the projected impacts. This is the power of geodesign for natural resource planning, which typically requires a strategy of adaptive management.

Figure 4.11: A braided stream of snowmelt winding its way through the valley. (Photo courtesy of Hamilton Greenwood)

Another benefit of EAGLES is the integration of scientific, domain-specific statistical analytics within the ArcGIS for Desktop platform. Species, habitat, and ecosystem modeling is based on complex system dynamics that often require analyses in statistical packages that run outside the GIS environment. But that's only part of the puzzle. When this data interacts with geospatial data, the synthesis of the various combinations and the visualization of the data over the landscape inform and improve the models. When changes to the landscape are proposed, or seen as inevitable, in the case of natural disturbances or climate change, alternative scenarios can be considered and plans put in place to minimize the projected impacts. This is the power of geodesign for natural resource planning, which typically requires a strategy of adaptive management.

As the degree of complexity in statistical analyses and remote sensing data increases, a set of standardized techniques and common data protocols becomes more essential, especially when supporting repeatable, transparent methods for ecological modeling. The successful intersection of these two domains requires workflow architectures that are simple enough to be widely adopted yet sophisticated enough to meet the criteria for decision-making standards. This requires a balance between high-level thinking of ecological pattern detection alongside the necessary attention to fine detail that allows researchers to model the ecological world accurately.

Finding solutions to major ecological challenges will require *new ways of thinking*. It is no longer humans *against* nature or humans *in* nature—it is humans *with* nature. Whether it's Yellowstone's pronghorn antelope, grizzly bear populations, or the collapse of Pacific Northwest salmon runs, science and GIS have lifted each of these issues—and many others like them—from subjective opinion and polarization to a place where decisions could be made on the basis of facts.

The work done by YERC is a significant contribution to the field of geodesign, which seeks to integrate the two most complex systems on earth—human social systems and ecological systems—directly into the acts of design and planning.

Key Links

Yellowstone Ecological Research Center
http://www.yellowstoneresearch.org/index.html

Yellowstone National Park
http://www.nps.gov/yell/index.htm

NASA
http://www.nasa.gov/

US Fish and Wildlife Service
http://www.fws.gov/

Acknowledgments

Special thanks to Robert Crabtree, Jennifer Sheldon, Brandt Winkelman, Yellowstone Ecological Research Center, and P.J. White, Yellowstone National Park. A good deal of the chapter content came from the *EAGLES User Manual*.[9] Thanks also to Hamilton Greenwood for permission to use his lovely photographs of species, adding greater meaning and context to the chapter.

Notes and References

[1] Paul Schullery, *Searching for Yellowstone: Ecology and Wonder in the Last Wilderness* (New York: Mariner Books, 1999), 7.

[2] Native American Tribes of Montana website, http://www.native-languages.org/montana.htm.

[3] "Yellowstone National Park," UNESCO World Heritage Centre web page. Retrieved May 6, 2011, from http://whc.unesco.org/en/list/28.

[4] Yellowstone Ecological Research Center website. Retrieved May 11, 2011, from http://www.yellowstoneresearch.org/about_mission.html.

[5] J. Beel, B. Gipp, and C. Müller. "'SciPlore MindMapping'—A Tool for Creating Mind Maps Combined with PDF and Reference Management," *D-Lib Magazine*, November/December 2009.

[6] Net primary production is the rate at which all the plants in an ecosystem produce net useful chemical energy. Retrieved May 16, 2011, from http://en.wikipedia.org/wiki/Primary_production#GPP_and_NPP.

[7] EAGLES geospatial wiki, http://geospatialdatawiki.wikidot.com/.

[8] COASTER, http://www.coasterdata.net/.

[9] K. R. Manlove, D. J. Weiss, and J. W. Sheldon, *EAGLES User Manual* (Bozeman, MT: Yellowstone Ecological Research Center, 2011). Retrieved May 16, 2011, from http://www.yellowstoneresearch.org/download/EAGLES_Manual.pdf.

5

Singapore's Sustainable Development

"A unique lakeside destination for business and leisure."

Urban Redevelopment Authority (URA), 2008

The Republic of Singapore is a city-state composed of 63 islands off the southern tip of the Malay Peninsula. It is highly urbanized with approximately 5.1 million people (as of 2010) living in an area that covers approximately 270 square miles. By comparison, the city of San Diego has a population of 1.3 million living over 340 square miles. Singapore has finite space, limited water supplies, and no natural resources. Nearly everything in Singapore is imported, whether it is for personal consumption, manufacturing, or construction. This makes Singapore highly susceptible to market fluctuations, especially in fossil fuels. The government of Singapore has made sustainable development, the use of renewable energy, and the efficient use of resources primary considerations in all future planning efforts.

Every 10 years, as part of Concept Plan review, Singapore reevaluates its long-term land-use strategies to ensure that there is sufficient land to meet anticipated population and economic growth needs without damaging the environment.[1] Given that the high concentration of commercial activities in the city center and infrastructure constraints make its continued growth untenable, a strategy of decentralization is actively being pursued. In the Master Plan 2008, the Urban Redevelopment Authority (URA), the national land-use planning authority of Singapore, heralded the Jurong Lake District (JLD) as a suitable place to build a new regional center to support economic activities outside the central business district, referring to it as "a unique lakeside destination for business and leisure."[2] To help with this complex planning effort, URA would use ArcGIS to model, visualize, and communicate the advantages of alternative scenarios.

JLD comprises two distinct but complementary precincts totaling 360 hectares (ha): a commercial hub at Jurong Gateway and a vibrant world-class leisure destination at Lakeside. With the Jurong East mass rapid transit (MRT) interchange station as its hub, the 70 ha Jurong Gateway is planned to be the largest commercial area outside the city center. When fully developed, it will provide more than 500,000 square meters of office space and 250,000 square meters of retail, food and beverage, entertainment, and other complementary uses including 1,000 new homes. This will provide opportunities for people to live, work, and play in the same area. Jurong Lakeside, which will comprise 220 ha of land and 70 ha of water body, will be transformed into an exciting destination for locals and tourists, with plans to develop four or five family-friendly attractions and some 2,800 hotel rooms to meet increased demand.[3] Recreational amenities, such as parks, park connectors, boardwalks, and wetlands, will also be built around the scenic lake. The two precincts will be seamlessly integrated. Pedestrians

Figure 5.1: Skyline of Singapore's business district. (Image copyright oksana.perkins, 2011; used under license from Shutterstock.com)

Overall, the aim is to formulate a holistic framework to guide the planning, design, and development of the Jurong Lake District, one that considers the environment, the economy, and society concurrently during the decision-making process.

can walk conveniently in all-weather comfort from the Jurong East MRT station to most developments and public facilities in Jurong Gateway and Lakeside through an extensive network of landscaped malls and elevated pedestrian walkways.

As outlined in Singapore's Blueprint for Sustainable Development, unveiled by the Inter-Ministerial Committee on Sustainable Development (IMCSD), JLD will be developed as one of Singapore's new sustainable high-density districts.[4] Overall, the aim is to formulate a holistic framework to guide the planning, design, and development of the Jurong Lake District, one that considers the environment, the economy, and society concurrently during the decision-making process.

URA proactively included aspects of the sustainability blueprint in the JLD planning efforts, such as the incorporation of landscaped open space and pedestrian park connectors to heighten the sense of greenery and closeness to nature; increase accessibility to existing transit, public facilities, and venues; and encourage people to walk, bike, and use public transportation. Land sale requirements were also put in place to mandate that developers achieve higher Building Construction Authority (BCA) Green Mark[5] environmental impact and performance ratings for new buildings

> "To achieve balance and efficiency when confronting the complexity in, and interaction between, the various natural and man-made systems, the concept of integrated design helps link together what conventional planning and engineering methods deal with separately."
>
> Brown and Kellenberg, 2010

(minimum Platinum rating for public buildings and minimum GoldPlus rating for private developments). Additional initiatives require 100 percent replacement of greenery lost to development and promote "skyrise" greenery—the addition of elevated parks, gardens, and green roofs on rooftops and skyways; the protection and enhancement of biodiversity; the reduction of resource use through building rehabilitation; and the increase of water catchment and treatment using natural systems whenever possible. But how were these visionary goals going to be evaluated and translated into reality given the myriad of stakeholders, assortment of variables, and budgetary constraints?

To assist with this ambitious plan, URA enlisted the help of AECOM, which proposed the use of a geodesign framework using ArcGIS to help organize and address the complex sustainability needs for such a large-scale project like JLD. The geodesign framework provides a whole-systems thinking approach that integrates land use, infrastructure, ecology, and building principles with cultural values through a modeling platform to evaluate and compare the combined impact of any number of alternative design scenarios.

The Sustainable Systems Integration Model

The Sustainable Systems Integration Model (or SSIM) is a key component of AECOM's sustainability planning process, providing a platform for rationally evaluating, balancing, and costing a wide variety of sustainability strategies to determine the combination best suited for the economic, social, and business objectives of a given project (figure 5.2). "SSIM places ecological enhancement and service components side by side with energy, water, mobility, green building,

and sociocultural strategies so that a truly integrated, balanced sustainability program can be measured and conceived" (Brown and Kellenberg 2010).[6] The result is a whole-system economic and GIS evaluation tool developed to work at multiple scales.

SSIM is often described as a *sustainability framework* composed of many steps and modeling techniques that allow users to select the themes and variables most befitting a given project's needs. The framework tracks a set of indicators including total energy use, water demand, waste produced, vehicle miles traveled, and total greenhouse gas emissions that can be modeled to show the impact of a single building, block of buildings, or entire community. Various energy or water conservation strategies can be recombined and modeled to show the immediate carbon or water footprint, as well as initial development costs or ongoing maintenance and management costs of a given scheme for any point in the future.[7]

Stage 1—Urban Form and Master Planning

"SSIM starts by using a GIS-based modeling tool to compare sustainability merits of (various) alternative urban form solutions" (Kellenberg and Walters 2010).[8] Urban form, the physical layout and design of a city, including land use and circulation patterns, has the largest impact on a city's energy use and GHG emissions.[9] Stage 1 seeks to identify the best mix of urban form, land-use density, and transportation network to achieve the highest trip capture and reduction in carbon emissions at the lowest cost. This stage encompasses what would be considered the 10 percent design phase, covered by strategic planning, predesign, and the

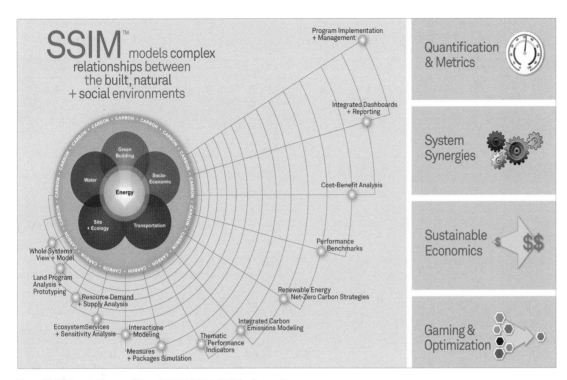

SSIM™ models complex relationships between the built, natural + social environments

Program Implementation + Management

Integrated Dashboards + Reporting

Cost-Benefit Analysis

Performance Benchmarks

Renewable Energy Net-Zero Carbon Strategies

Integrated Carbon Emissions Modeling

Thematic Performance Indicators

Measures + Packages Simulation

Interactions Modeling

EcosystemServices + Sensitivity Analysis

Resource Demand + Supply Analysis

Land Program Analysis + Prototyping

Whole Systems View + Model

Green Building — Socio-Economic — Transportation — Site + Ecology — Water — Energy — CARBON

Quantification & Metrics

System Synergies

Sustainable Economics

Gaming & Optimization

Figure 5.2: SSIM model diagram. (Figure © 2011 AECOM. All Rights Reserved)

selection of master plan alternatives. But first, the geographic context and key processes have to be clarified and understood as they will form the basis for evaluation of the current state and proposed changes.

The process started out with a visioning workshop at which all stakeholders and subject experts were brought together to help define and prioritize issues, metrics, and target goals. In this case, the stakeholders were the URA, National Water Agency (PUB), Land Transport Authority (LTA), National Parks Board (NParks), and Building Construction Authority, among others. Participants were encouraged to address problems beyond their fields of expertise. The end result of this dynamic interaction and the

sharing of views and perspectives across disciplines was an increased understanding among stakeholders of the complexity of key issues, enabling them to reach agreement on priorities and possible solutions.

For JLD, the primary systems or themes (*process models*) that needed to be understood and evaluated were organized into a preliminary sustainability framework matrix:

- Urban form and design

- Transportation

- Ecological systems

- Sociocultural infrastructure

"SSIM starts by using a GIS-based modeling tool to compare sustainability merits of (various) alternative urban form solutions."

Kellenberg and Walters, 2010

59

Key performance indicators (KPIs) on such topics as carbon footprint, energy, biodiversity, potable water, and transportation were defined to assist in measuring resource efficiency, performance, and cumulative impact of each system.

- Energy (residential building, retail building, office building, hotel building, civic building, and public realm)

- Green buildings

- Water

- Waste

- Noise

For each of these primary systems, objectives were identified as well as strategies to help achieve each objective. Key performance indicators (KPIs) on such topics as carbon footprint, energy, biodiversity, potable water, and transportation were defined to assist in measuring resource efficiency, performance, and cumulative impact of each system. In addition to the above,

an initial ranking of priority was determined based on discussions with the URA and the relevant agencies. The last item on the matrix was a range of performance targets for each system. This range was a temporary mechanism to allow the performance of *aspirational targets* of a desired future to be put in relative perspective with business as usual (BAU), especially regarding initial costs and cost-benefit.

The next step in the process was a *gap analysis* or the identification of the differences between the current master plan's sustainability performance and that proposed by the aspirational targets. The KPIs of each primary system in the existing plan were quantified by modeling techniques appropriate for each system. In some cases, the existing KPI was more qualitative such as with noise and sociocultural components.

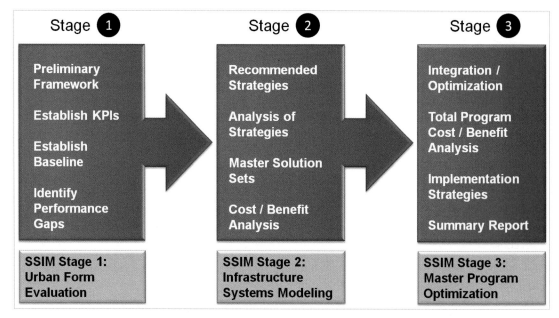

Figure 5.3: SSIM takes stakeholders through three stages organized around (1) urban form and design, (2) infrastructure or primary systems modeling, and (3) master program optimization. (Figure © 2011 AECOM. All Rights Reserved)

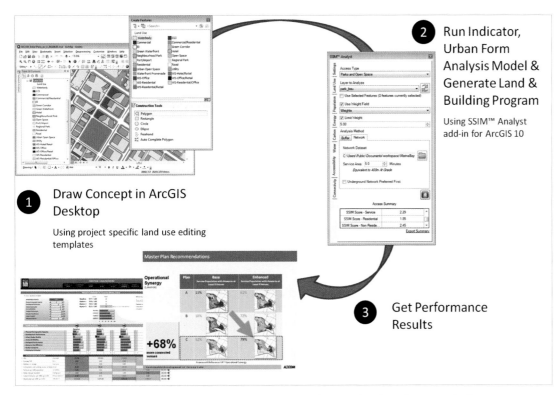

1 Draw Concept in ArcGIS Desktop

Using project specific land use editing templates

2 Run Indicator, Urban Form Analysis Model & Generate Land & Building Program

Using SSIM™ Analyst add-in for ArcGIS 10

3 Get Performance Results

Figure 5.4: SSIM conceptual workflow diagram makes extensive use of ArcGIS ModelBuilder, Network Analyst, and a customized toolset. (Figure © 2011 AECOM. All Rights Reserved)

The next step in the process was a gap analysis or the identification of the differences between the current master plan's sustainability performance and that proposed by the aspirational targets.

To create a relatively accurate frame of reference, the team established definitions for BAU and baseline to which the aspirational targets and all future scenarios could be compared to understand improvements in performance as well as associated costs (*evaluation models*). For JLD, BAU was defined as the original master plan in place for Jurong Gateway and Lakeside assuming conventional construction practices. The baseline was defined as the original master plan, combined with the existing sustainable development initiatives already implemented by URA such as Green Mark certification, the proposed elevated pedestrian network, and the greenery replacement program.

The gap analysis clarified the degree to which each system needed to be improved to meet the aspirational targets (figure 5.5). Over a several-month period, URA worked closely with an international team of AECOM sustainability experts, in collaboration with multiple public agencies, in developing key quantitative and qualitative measures to close the gaps. The JLD master plan formed the data backbone of both the BAU and baseline models (*representation models*). The main differences between the models were in the energy mandates that were assumed for each scenario according to the definitions outlined during the visioning workshop.

The gap analysis clarified the degree to which each system and its related issues would have to be improved to meet the aspirational targets.

Topic	KPI		Aspirational Targets	GAP
Land Use Balance	% Local Trip Capture		30%	15%
Access to Parks	% Service Population with Access to at Least 1 Park		80%	32%
Access to Local Services	% Service Population with Access to at Least 1 Local Service	Retail	85%	15%
		Medical	45%	8%
Shading	% of pedestrian space with shade coverage (build/landscape shade)		80%	25%
Place Making (Gateway)	% Service Population with Access to at Least 1 Quality Gathering Place		75%	49%
Ecological Integration	Average area of connected parks		26ha	4ha
Operational Synergy (Lakeside)	% Service Population with Access at Least 3 Venues			
Urban Heat Island	Improvement on external thermal comfort level (Actual Sensation Vote – ASV)		2%	2%
	Reduce in urban heat island intensity		-1.0 degC	-1.0 degC
Carbon Footprint	% of carbon emission reduction		23%	4%

Figure 5.5: The KPI for each topic and aspirational targets and the gap between business as usual and the aspirational targets helped clarify where to focus change initiatives. (Figure © 2011 AECOM. All Rights Reserved)

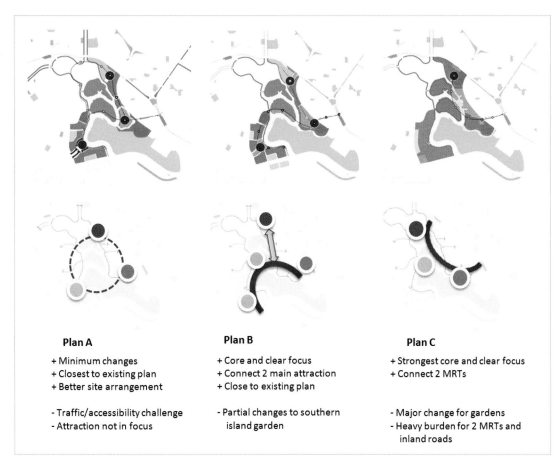

Plan A

+ Minimum changes
+ Closest to existing plan
+ Better site arrangement

- Traffic/accessibility challenge
- Attraction not in focus

Plan B

+ Core and clear focus
+ Connect 2 main attraction
+ Close to existing plan

- Partial changes to southern
  island garden

Plan C

+ Strongest core and clear focus
+ Connect 2 MRTs

- Major change for gardens
- Heavy burden for 2 MRTs and
  inland roads

Alternative master plans were "sketched" by participants using customized templates or palettes of predetermined land uses, building types, transportation modes, community facilities, and other amenities.

Figure 5.6: An example of three alternative plans shown as A, B, and C along with their explanation. (Figure © 2011 AECOM. All Rights Reserved)

Once the BAU and baseline models were created, alternative master plans (*change models*) were "sketched" by participants using customized templates or palettes of predetermined land uses, building types, transportation modes, community facilities, and other amenities, to help facilitate this process (figure 5.6). Each palette type has its own assumptions outlining its spatial dimensions, land-use mixes, density, and a number of other parameters. GHG, water, waste, and energy use can be calculated for each building based on land-use type, floor area, density, and building material and sustainability guidelines. This palette helped users sketch a number of alternative scenarios with associated impacts for comparison against the BAU and baseline plans. Sketching was facilitated using the standard ArcGIS editing template functionality.

SSIM GIS mapping and geoprocessing tools, developed as an ArcGIS for Desktop add-in using

63

The alternative master plans were evaluated against key performance indicators, allowing participants to actually see the impact of their design decisions just by running the tool. Plan C performed the best.

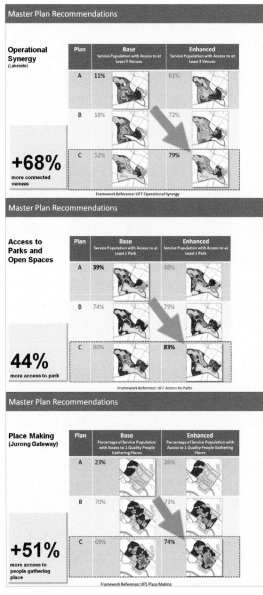

Figure 5.7: Here are a few examples of the spatial analyses performed to show the impact of plan changes on different indicators important to the stakeholders. Heat maps created using ArcGIS for Desktop show colors from red to yellow to green indicating good, better, best for each plan. Plan C shows the highest benefit for each of these indicators. (Figure © 2011 AECOM. All Rights Reserved)

ArcObjects, were used to model accessibility to certain plan features including land-use spatial allocation, internal and external connectivity, and access to key services and transit. Proximity analyses were performed within the SSIM add-in's custom interface using ArcGIS Network Analyst to measure actual pathway distance, as opposed to a straight, as-the-crow-flies buffer analysis. A unique addition to the JLD project was the creation of tools to measure the accessibility of vertical components, such as elevated parks, skyways, and trams. These *evaluation models*, characteristic of the geodesign, quickly evaluated design decisions, allowing participants to see the impact just by running the tool (figure 5.7).

Using a combination of spatial and statistical models, the strengths and weakness of the existing plan were identified and changes were made to improve carbon footprint, trip capture, connectivity, land-use balance, amount of open space, ecology, and so on. This was accomplished using the existing URA master plan as a base case and then calibrating the model with improvements through multiple iterations until two refined scenarios were developed. Based on the outputs of these *impact models*, modifications and improvements to both the master plan and land-use program were achieved, narrowing the gaps between the existing plan and the aspirational targets identified earlier. The primary areas of improvement were related to reductions in vehicle kilometers traveled (VKT) through realignment of roadways and improved connectivity and synergy between major venues and attractions.

Stage II—Infrastructure or Primary Systems Evaluation and Modeling

After a preferred master plan framework was selected, a more intensive evaluation of sustainability practices and measures took place with a greater focus on a detailed infrastructure level of analysis. By tweaking certain measures—for example, the selection of certain building materials or switching to low-flow faucets—additional improvements can be made in water consumption, energy consumption, or cost. This step seeks to answer three core questions for each theme: (1) What energy reduction targets should be evaluated? (2) Which combination of project design features is required to achieve each target? and (3) Which combination of project design features would achieve the reduction targets in the most cost-effective manner? The submodels developed for each core theme push for increasingly higher levels of resource efficiency while tracking the conceptual cost and environmental benefit of each solution set:

- Residential building energy

- Retail building energy

- Office building energy

- Industrial building energy

- Water—domestic, storm, waste, recycled, and gray

- Transportation

- Green building

- Public realm energy

- Ecological systems and open space planning

- Sociocultural infrastructure

- Urban heat islands

Just like in the evaluation of urban form in stage I, stage II requires the identification of a BAU and baseline for each system (the former being the minimum level of performance allowed by building and zoning codes while the latter represents the level of performance required by URA in the existing plan). The primary difference between these two was in the amount of open space and green building requirements in the Gateway district. Three additional levels of performance (termed good, better, best) that had been earlier identified in the sustainability framework matrix were the basis for assembling "packages" of measures that would theoretically achieve each of the respective targets for each system. These packages were then modeled to test whether they, in fact, achieved the targets. Where models were not applicable or within the scope of the project, manual calculations were used. If the packages of measures did not achieve the desired target, they were adjusted until they came close enough to be considered in compliance. This approach created a robust selection of measure packages that could be (1) evaluated for economic efficiency and (2) used in the final stage of the process to assemble a master sustainability program that met the overall economic criteria for the project.

Cost-Benefit Analysis

After identification of the packages of measures to be utilized in closing the gap between the aspirational targets and the current BAU case, each package of strategies underwent a cost estimating step and then a cost-benefit analysis. This information allowed further refinement of the packages so that those moving forward would be the most effective from a cost impact standpoint. Further, the cost-benefit data would allow the stage III total program optimization step to achieve the

After a preferred master plan was selected, a more intensive evaluation of sustainability practices and measures took place, focusing on the details of building performance.

highest level of cost-effectiveness. Economic measurements were defined at a conceptual level for each component, appropriate for strategic planning of this kind. The following economic information was typical for most of the systems analyzed:

- Capital cost

- Operating cost and possible savings

- Percent performance improvement per $1,000 invested

- Metric tons of CO_2e reduction per $1,000 invested

- Simple payback period

- Discounted payback period (life cycle cost analysis based)

- Return on investment

- Net cash flow

- Ratio of % increased cost to % increased performance

Stage III—Master Program Optimization

The goal of SSIM stage III is to combine the effects of multiple systems and strategies to create *integrated sustainability programs* for each of the *alternative master plan scenarios* refined in stage I across the entire project site. This is facilitated by a unique tool called the Gameboard that allows the selection of a performance package for each major system and simultaneously reports various performance and cost indicators resulting from the package selections (see figure 5.8). AECOM designed the Gameboard using the commercially

available Risk Solver Platform for Excel. The SSIM Gameboard is used to optimize the overall master sustainability program. In this context, *optimization* is the process of selecting unique combinations of sustainability choices that result in achieving the aspirational targets set out in stage I using a set of predetermined cost thresholds. The optimization process is assisted by a logic engine that solves for the set of constraints stipulated by the thresholds.

In the end, three to five master sustainability framework programs were defined and evaluated. The variation between the programs included multiple combinations of good/better/best scenarios on all of the systems. Each master program solved for optimal scenarios regarding total district carbon, energy, VKT, and water reduction. For each potential framework program, the following were calculated and compared:

Key Performance Indicators

- Total domestic water demand reduction

- Total residential building energy reduction

- Total commercial building energy reduction

- Total public realm energy reduction

- Total reduction in VKT

- Total reduction in GHG emissions

Cost/Savings Indicators

- Total initial project costs/savings

- Total ongoing monthly project costs/savings

- Initial costs/savings to residential buildings in cost/square mile and % over base costs

In this context, optimization is the process of selecting unique combinations of sustainability choices that result in achieving the aspirational targets set out in stage I using a set of predetermined cost thresholds.

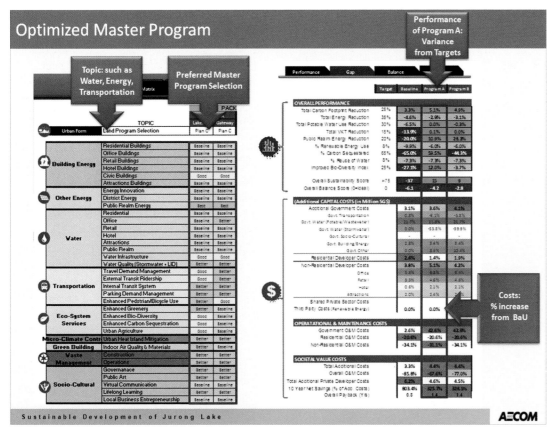

Figure 5.8: The SSIM Gameboard allows stakeholders to "play" with the values of different indicators until the optimal balance of performance and cost is achieved. (Figure © 2011 AECOM. All Rights Reserved)

The stage III evaluation helped identify a combination of packages that achieved all the aspirational targets and exceeded several ecology-related targets while keeping within the cost thresholds identified with URA.

- Initial costs/savings to nonresidential buildings in cost/square mile and % over base costs

- Life cycle costs/savings to master developer

- Life cycle costs/savings to third-party energy or infrastructure financing entity

- Life cycle costs/savings to residential buildings in cost/square mile and % over base costs

- Life cycle costs/savings to nonresidential buildings in cost/square mile and % over base costs

Discussion

The stage III evaluation helped identify a combination of packages that achieved all the aspirational targets and exceeded several ecology-related targets while keeping within the cost thresholds identified with URA that were generally within

67

	Retail Buildings	Baseline	Baseline
	Hotel Buildings	Baseline	Baseline
	Civic Buildings	Best	Good
	Attractions Buildings	Baseline	Baseline
Other Energy	Energy Innovation	Baseline	Baseline
	District Energy	Baseline	Baseline
	Public Realm Energy	Best	Best
Water	Residential	Better	Better
	Office	Better	Better
	Retail	Better	Better
	Hotel	Better	Better
	Attractions	Better	Better
	Public Realm	Better	Better
	Water Infrastructure	Baseline	Baseline
	Water Quality (Stormwater + LID)	Better	Better
Transportation	Travel Demand Management	Good	Better
	External Transit Ridership	Good	Better
	Internal Transit System	Better	Better
	Parking Demand Management	Better	Better
	Enhanced Pedestrian/ Bicycle Use	Better	Good
Eco-Systems	Enhanced Greenery	Better	Baseline
	Enhanced Bio-Diversity	Good	Baseline
	Enhanced Carbon Sequestration	Good	Baseline
	Urban Agriculture	Good	Baseline
Micro-Climate Control	Urban Heat Island Mitigation	Better	Better
Green Building	Indoor Air Quality & Materials	Better	Baseline
		Better	Better

Figure 5.9: Example of an SSIM Gameboard model run comparing impacts of design decisions against KPIs. (Figure © 2011 AECOM. All Rights Reserved)

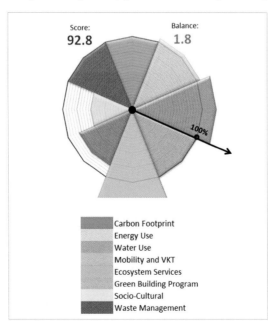

Figure 5.10: Example of a final balance rosette, part of the SSIM toolset. (Figure © 2011 AECOM. All Rights Reserved)

public- and private-sector market parameters (*impact models*).

Each model run results in a series of outputs that synthesize the data into easy-to-understand graphics, two of which are the Gameboard (figure 5.9) and the rosette (figure 5.10). The Gameboard shows the urban form themes and systems subcategories listed and colored to thematically match the rosette. The packages were nominally labeled Baseline, Good, Better, and Best and color-coded from gray to yellow to green to increase readability and quick assessment of status. These provide a valuable feedback mechanism that facilitates progressive design iterations to assist stakeholders with the comparison of alternatives and ultimately decision making (*decision models*).

To ensure that the preferred sustainability program is well balanced relative to the various dimensions of healthy community and environment, the level of improvement in the primary systems was compared en masse on the rosette, allowing relative shortfalls to become visible.

The SSIM tool allowed the URA to examine theoretical 10-year life cycle analysis comparing net present value for each model run. Due to the confidential nature of the project, the dollar amounts could not be shared here. But in a number of well-documented cases around the globe, the savings from energy and water efficiency are able to offset the investments in other sectors such as parks and open space, protection of biodiversity, public transportation, potable water infrastructure, and even social programs.[10]

The refined *sustainability framework matrix* serves as the master checklist for achieving a holistic sustainability program for JLD. It is a living document that will be amended as time goes on and as adjustments need to be made in targets, due to changes in either technology, demographics, costs, or priorities. In this way, it becomes a tool for adaptive management throughout the development project's life cycle.

Lessons Learned

The Jurong Lake District case study demonstrated an admirable usage of the geodesign framework and introduced a number of enabling technologies. The many benefits of the approach included:

Scalability—Being able to track and evaluate performance at a building, parcel, or city level is crucial in today's world as cities strive to meet GHG reduction goals. SSIM has the granularity to measure potential design performance at various scales, rolling up total carbon to create a citywide carbon footprint. No longer can a building be constructed without taking into account the impact on the whole.

Self-mitigating—Typically, master plan alternatives are developed and evaluated and a final plan selected independently from environmental assessment. The environmental impact report (EIR) process takes time and often results in an imperfect compromise with mitigation as part of the solution. By evaluating a master plan along with infrastructure and a sustainability framework in progress, the resulting master plan can self-correct to avoid unnecessary impacts to the environment that could result in costly mitigation.

Holistic approach—The system allows the evaluation of multiple systems within a common framework. Land use, building types, transportation, water, waste, open space, health, sense of place, and many more, can all be evaluated together, providing a synergy that could otherwise be missed in more traditional design approaches.

Return on investment—One of the key benefits of SSIM is that it allows users to see and evaluate the cost implications of their choices. Many would like to go entirely green, but often the costs of going green are more than the market can bear. By including costs in the evaluation, the element of surprise is taken out of the equation, increasing the likelihood of successful implementation.

Visual storytelling—The highly graphic and visual approach helps make complex data and statistical patterns visible and easy to understand. This is particularly important when engaging stakeholders or other broad audiences.

As a final note, it is the hope of all involved that the assessment and selection of key design elements will have a positive impact on what is ultimately built. Identifying key governmental or private entities tasked with the responsibility of final decision making and ultimately with program implementation is crucial. This project did just that.

Following this up with design packages that include best practices for sustainable construction including building materials, fixtures, and so forth, is equally important. Including these directly in the contract language is key, as is offering training, guidance, and oversight to make sure contractors comply with the best practices. Given the holistic nature of the sustainability framework elements, only a joint collaborative effort between all participants will lead to full success and implementation of the recommended program.

Geodesign lets you integrate environmental assessment into the design process in real time, resulting in a self-correcting design that reduces or avoids costly mitigation altogether.

Key Links

Urban Redevelopment Authority
http://www.ura.gov.sg/

PUB National Water Agency
http://www.pub.gov.sg/Pages/default.aspx

Land Transport Authority
http://www.lta.gov.sg/

National Parks
http://www.nparks.gov.sg/cms/

Building Construction Authority
http://www.bca.gov.sg/

AECOM
http://www.aecom.com

Acknowledgments

Special thanks to Matthew Palavido, AECOM, for contributions and review. Additional thanks go to the project's sponsors that include Singapore's Urban Redevelopment Authority, National Water Agency, Land Transport Authority, National Parks, and Building Construction Authority.

A number of case study details came from the Jurong Lake Sustainability Assessment Framework Summary Report, Revision 2, dated March 2011.

Notes and References

1 "Master Plan 2008," Urban Redevelopment Authority. Retrieved June 22, 2011, from http://www.ura.gov.sg/MP2008/intro.htm.

2 Urban Redevelopment Authority, "Blueprint for Jurong Unveiled," news release, April 4, 2008. Retrieved June 10, 2011, from http://www.ura.gov.sg/pr/text/2008/pr08-38.html.

3 Urban Redevelopment Authority, "URA Launches Draft Master Plan 2008: Where My Future Is: Great Opportunities, Good Life," news release, May 23, 2008. Retrieved June 10, 2011, from http://www.ura.gov.sg/pr/text/2008/pr08-55.html.

4 Inter-Ministerial Committee on Sustainable Development, A Lively and Liveable Singapore: Strategies for Sustainable Growth (Ministry of the Environment and Water Resources and Ministry of National Development, 2009). Retrieved June 10, 2011, from http://app.mewr.gov.sg/data/ImgCont/1292/sustainbleblueprint_forweb.pdf.

5 The Singapore government's Building and Construction Authority developed Green Mark, a green building rating system used to help evaluate a building on its environmental impact and performance. It is endorsed and supported by the National Environment Agency. It provides a comprehensive framework for assessing the overall environmental performance of new and existing buildings to promote sustainable design, construction, and operations practices in buildings. More information can be found at http://www.bca.gov.sg/greenmark/green_mark_criteria.html.

6 Isaac Brown and Steve Kellenberg, "Ecologically Engineering Cities through Integrated Sustainable Systems Planning," Journal of Green Building 4, no. 1 (Winter 2010): 1–18 (Glen Allen, VA: College Publishing). Retrieved June 16, 2011, from http://ed.edaw.com/eNewsData/articleDocuments/89442_brown,kellenberg_journlofgrnbuilding.pdf.

7 Steve Kellenberg and Honey Walters, "Measuring Carbon Performance and Climate Stable Practice," in Climate Design: Design and Planning for the Age of Climate Change (Singapore: ORO Editions, 2010), 132–139.

8 Ibid.

9 Jonathan Norman, Heather L. MacLean, and Christopher A. Kennedy, "Comparing High and Low Residential Density: Life-Cycle Analysis of Energy Use and Greenhouse Gas Emissions," Journal of Urban Planning and Development, March 2006, American Society of Civil Engineers (ASCE). Retrieved June 21, 2011, from http://www.sb4all.org/uploads/Comparing_High_and_Low_Resedential_Density_Life_Cycle_Analysis_-_Energy_Use_and_Greenhouse_Gas_Emmissions.pdf.

10 ICLEI Global, "Best Municipal Practices for Energy Efficiency," chap. 7.0 in Profiting from Energy Efficiency. Retrieved December 2011 from http://www.iclei.org/index.php?id=1677.

6

Building Smart from the Ground Up

Geodesign brought value to each stage of the facility life cycle from site analytics and design to planning and construction, as well as operations, security, and sustainability.

Sabah Al-Salem University—Kuwait University City

Kuwait University (KU) was established in October 1966, five years after Kuwait's independence from the British. Over the years, it has developed into a large, well-respected public university with over 20,000 students and over 1,000 faculty. [1] The only problem is that the campuses are dispersed throughout the city with difficulties to expand to meet the educational needs of an ever-increasing student body.

To meet this need, Kuwait University has embarked on one of the most ambitious campus development projects in the world. The massive Sabah Al-Salem University City—Kuwait University is being designed and built from the ground up and will emerge from the desert over the next four years as part of a multibillion-dollar development initiative. [2] The new university plays a pivotal role in Kuwait's strategy of diversification and the development of a knowledge-based economy.

The new 490-hectare (1,211-acre) Sabah Al-Salem University City—Kuwait University will consolidate six different campuses, 16 colleges, [3] dormitories, parking, and support facilities, all expected to accommodate 40,000 full-time students by 2025. [4] Master planning presented a variety of challenges, including responding to difficult climatic conditions, ensuring site security, and meeting sustainability guidelines.

To meet those challenges, Kuwait University chose to apply the geospatial concepts typically discussed in its GIS courses to support the entire process of designing, building, and operating the huge new University City. In early 2010, Kuwait University recognized a need for specialized consulting to help create a GIS implementation road map that would support the vision of the Sabah Al-Salem University City—Kuwait University project. For the plan to be successful, the needs of both Kuwait University and the contracted project management company (Turner Projacs) would have to be incorporated.

Those needs included using geodesign processes in novel ways to bring value to each stage of the facility life cycle from site analytics and design to planning and construction, as well as operations, security, and sustainability. This ambitious endeavor had to overcome many challenges, both technical and cultural, and represented a level of enterprise data development sorely missing in the multidisciplinary design, build, and operate world of today. The widespread use of ArcGIS as an enterprise GIS platform made it a natural place to start framing system architecture to support full facility life cycle management.

The goals of the project included establishing a powerful GIS for the new university based on a comprehensive geodatabase that would support multiple applications across the campus and be capable of scaling up as the project grew. ArcGIS for Server and ArcGIS for Desktop, along with many web applications created with ArcGIS Viewer for Silverlight, shall be used to monitor construction and provide a platform for future geospatial needs including the management of campus assets.

Modeling and Storing Data for an Entire Campus

From a geodesign perspective, one of the major challenges was defining data *representation models* and sound workflow integration between CAD and GIS data to support the full life cycle vision. This required examining the needs of each work stage, from concept to detailed design and construction to operations.

The master plan data was inherently conceptual, a general layout of block buildings, roads, landscaping, and grand themes to guide design. At the start of the project, this data formed the base layers of the GIS helping to support early site planning and logistics. Selected features like the site infrastructure, buildings, and building spaces were extracted from the design CAD drawings for use in the GIS to support construction management, quality assurance, clash detection, logistics, and the monitoring of progress.

Detailed design data for each building is inherently much more detailed, created to support actual construction. As-builts were to be submitted in both CAD and geodatabase format that must comply with the data model requirements, which include a large set of geometry and attribute data of interest for use in GIS.

A much more extensive range of features, including the detailed locations and characteristics of facilities and assets, will be captured from the as-built drawing information as each part of the new campus is finalized and commissioned. The final geodatabase created during this stage will include all the essential features needed to support the final operations stage of project development.

The entire facilities information infrastructure model required setting CAD and geodatabase design guidelines that all design firms would be required to follow so that drawing files could be quickly integrated into the master GIS geodatabase upon delivery. In turn, the GIS would be linked to the project management and document and drawing management systems to support monitoring and reporting of construction progress and change management across the entire site.

What makes this particular geodatabase unique is that it had to span features indoors and outdoors, underground and above, permanent and temporal. The process that ensued was a major effort that brought international experts across domains and professions to the table to design a unique, world-class GIS data model capable of supporting the full facility life cycle.

Master Plan Support

Coordinating a design and construction job of this size and duration requires a small army of dedicated experts and many years of planning and revisions. The project has engaged firms from around the world to design specialized structures for the 100-plus proposed buildings on campus. The master planning process is one of the first places where geodesign played an integral role, optimizing program elements and unifying the designs from individual bid packages into a single

From a geodesign perspective, one of the major challenges was defining data *representation models* and sound workflow integration between CAD and GIS data to support the full life cycle vision.

What makes this particular geodatabase unique is that it had to span features indoors and outdoors, underground and above, permanent and temporal.

Through the use of GIS, team members can now retrieve, update, and analyze construction logistics and daily operations across the campus through a simple web viewer.

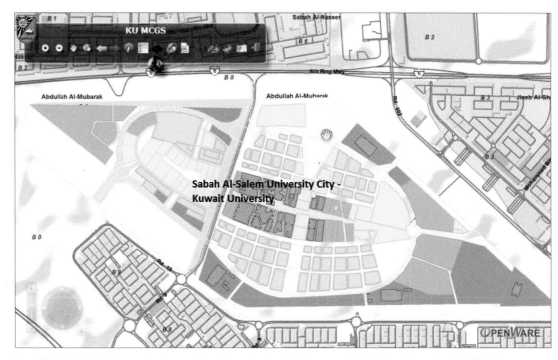

Figure 6.1: Kuwait University's master plan viewer provides a rich user interface, allowing access to detailed information on hundreds of buildings, construction phasing, bid packages, and key details to support design coordination, master plan optimization, and construction logistics. (Image by OpenWare, copyright, Kuwait University, 2011; all rights reserved; data courtesy of Kuwait University)

seamless view. By doing so, planners and decision makers can recognize design impacts and understand considerations that would be missed without a holistic understanding of the sum of the design parts. Some of the most compelling examples of the benefits of geodesign *process* and *evaluation modeling* included viewshed analysis from both ground vantage points and individual office windows, drainage, security planning, and solar aspect/radiation modeling. Esri technology allowed the team to do this by visualizing, analyzing, and querying the data in 2D and 3D, both important at different points in the master planning process.

Construction Management and Planning Support

At the peak of construction, there will be more than 10,000 construction personnel on-site daily and thousands of vehicle trips requiring access to building sites for deliveries. The construction management team is a seasoned group of professionals that has traditionally worked through planning and daily operations using paper drawings and markup pens. Through the use of GIS, team members can now retrieve, update, and analyze construction logistics and scheduling data, temporary staging locations and assignments, and daily operations across the entire campus through a simple web viewer. Daily stand-up meetings

Figure 6.2: The Silverlight viewer above shows a stockpile area being drawn, shown here as red line work. (Image by OpenWare, copyright, Kuwait University, 2011; all rights reserved; data courtesy of Kuwait University)

The geodesign *change* and *impact modeling* processes include room for adaptive management that allows design changes and impact assessment mid-implementation, ensuring goals are met.

utilize this information through the Construction Management viewer and allow quick sketching and markup, which is printed and taken to the field. This quick temporal snapshot helps meet the demands of the day, as well as the longer-term planning activities, to make construction logistics run smoothly.

As many a construction manager can attest, construction implementation rarely occurs without the need for a design change. This is very common on large construction efforts when teams realize midstream they've missed something very important like an existing utility easement, or a new technological advancement comes out that greatly reduces a particular design constraint. The geodesign *change* and *impact modeling* processes include room for *adaptive management* that allows design changes and impact assessment midimplementation to ensure that program goals are met and the design change has no unforeseen impact on other design elements.

Equally important is the visualization of construction over time (4D). Construction managers and decision makers can view and identify spatiotemporal clashes, accessibility problems, and other logistical issues before they happen.

Status Monitoring and Reporting

A project this size is like a large three-dimensional chess game, a giant, complex moving puzzle. As the project progresses, verification and

Using the map as a dashboard, all progress reports provide a full project snapshot that can be easily understood by anyone on the project team.

Figure 6.3: The viewer shows the progress of the various stages of construction implementation. A slider bar allows all project teams to see the history of planned and completed work at any phase of the project. (Image by OpenWare, copyright, Kuwait University, 2011; all rights reserved; data courtesy of Kuwait University)

Figure 6.4: A particularly nice feature of managing a construction project in a GIS is the ability to include georeferenced photographs of events that occur on the project site. This kind of qualitative data helps decision makers understand exactly what the issue is so they can make faster decisions. The different colors of these simple building massing models indicate each building's stage of completion using a red-orange-yellow-blue color ramp, red signifying not yet started and blue signifying that the building has been completed and accepted. (Image by OpenWare, copyright, Kuwait University, 2011; all rights reserved; data courtesy of Kuwait University and USGS)

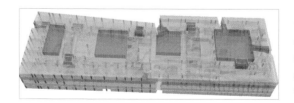

Figure 6.5: Space planning begins early for any building that has been incorporated into the facilities information infrastructure such as the new College of Education depicted here. (Image by OpenWare, copyright, Kuwait University, 2011; all rights reserved; data courtesy of Kuwait University)

monitoring of defined performance goals, risk, cost, and schedule—critical aspects of project controls—become increasingly important. Because so many tasks are dependent on other critical milestones, there needs to be a razor-sharp view of progress across all the ongoing activities. The GIS Reporting web application takes project assessment data from the tabular project report and displays it on the map, showing where activities are falling behind and which adjacent efforts might be impacted. This quick visual reporting style, using the map as a dashboard, accompanies all progress reports providing a full project snapshot that can be easily understood by anyone on the project team.

Another way of visualizing progress and key performance indicators is in a 3D GIS view of the campus. Using ArcGlobe services and ArcGIS Explorer, project leaders and executives can quickly get an up-to-date view of the building construction progress in 3D or request a high-level report (see figure 6.4).

Space Programming

While the campus buildings are not going to be completely finished and occupied for years, there is a requirement to begin the massive process of space programming for academic occupancy. As design details are delivered, floor plan data is readily made available in the GIS. This means that, prior to completion of construction, university staff can experiment with alternative space plan scenarios, assigning personnel and assets to define an optimal space utilization program. This also supports the validation of space requirements by size and type, as well as proximity to building services or required facilities. This can be done for each floor, across the entire building, and out to other buildings.

Figure 6.6: The Bedouin tent design dates back well over a thousand years. The tents were designed with one or more vents that could be opened to release hot air and keep the tent cool during hot weather, or closed to conserve heat during times of foul weather. (Image copyright Seleznev Oleg, 2011; used under license from Shutterstock.com)

Designing with Nature—a Sustainable Approach

Summer in Kuwait is long, very hot, and humid; daytime temperatures can rise to 145° F (61° C) with 85 percent humidity. The need for constant air conditioning is one of the greatest energy drains on the country. As a result, all KU buildings are designed to reflect environmental/sustainable performance equivalents to attaining a "silver" rating using the United States Green Building Council (USGBC) LEED[5] rating system by incorporating such enhancements as natural day lighting, photovoltaic solar panels, solar hot water heaters, wastewater recycling, superefficient mechanical systems, and sustainable materials.

Considering sun angle, solar gain, and natural shading in all aspects of design is an essential part of sustainable design. To make the most use of passive cooling, buildings are closely spaced to shade their neighbors in the morning and afternoon as much as possible.[6] Ingenious sunscreens protect windows from the summer heat while allowing filtered natural light to penetrate into classrooms, offices, and courtyards.

Some campus buildings, like the College of Arts building, even mimic the *al khaimah*, or Bedouin tent, with inward sloping walls and operable components that provide both natural shade and a chimney effect that creates natural updrafts to allow passive cooling to increase comfort and reduce energy use (see figure 6.7).[7]

Considering sun angle, solar gain, and natural shading in all aspects of design is an essential part of sustainable design.

79

Individual sustainable design elements add up, cumulatively ensuring that the master plan's programmatic goals on sustainability are achieved.

Figure 6.7: Sabah Al-Salem University City, College of Arts, demonstrates design ideally suited to the local environment. (Image courtesy of Perkins+Will)

Development of appropriate dry climate approaches to landscaping drives all landscaping aspects of the master plan. The extensive perimeter of the site has a continuous cover of indigenous vegetation highly adapted to the harsh climate and swelled landforms to enhance the capture of seasonal rains.[8]

Each of these individual sustainable design elements add up, cumulatively ensuring that the master plan's programmatic goals on sustainability are achieved both during construction and long after the buildings have been commissioned.

Discussion

Steinitz has described the geodesign framework as a broad set of social questions that walk decision makers through the process of landscape change, from condition assessment to the evaluation of alternative landscape change options.[9] His process requires at least three passes through a series of six questions, but the permutations can increase exponentially depending on the number of alternative scenarios and the variation of design elements within those alternatives. Implementation of a final design adds a whole other dimension to geodesign, that of *adaptive management*.[10] As many an architect or landscape architect knows, the work isn't over until the site is built, commissioned, and opened, and even then, changes can occur.

The Sabah Al-Salem University City—Kuwait University project is a multibillion-dollar, multiyear project. Changes of all kinds will occur before this project is over and all the buildings commissioned. A given change on a project this size could be minor, that is, occur within a building site's defined area so that it only affects one building or set of buildings, but other changes could ripple throughout many sites, even causing a redesign or review of an entire master plan as recently happened at Masdar City in Abu Dhabi.[11] At Sabah Al-Salem University City, geodesign impact evaluation processes performed during the initial design phase of the future Medical Campus caused the initial design to go through another round of master planning to ensure program goals were going to be met. Spatially enabling a change management plan using the geodesign framework can save substantial amounts of time and money throughout a project's life cycle.

The efficiencies gained by using ArcGIS as the information framework on which change can be managed is one of the benefits of geodesign. In this case, ArcGIS and geodesign were used to optimize and implement an ongoing and complex construction project that requires constant monitoring of a thousand moving pieces, the master geodatabase and GIS data model keeping track of data as it moves through the work stages—from conceptual and schematic to detailed design and as-built. Flexibility, adaptability, and countless alternative scenarios must be tracked and evaluated and their impact assessed every day, and geodesign processes are helping to make that happen.

Lessons Learned

The benefits of using geodesign processes to support facility life cycle management are numerous:

- Geodesign plays a significant role in the complex world of adaptive management throughout the construction process.

- The use of GIS strengthens and streamlines the design and construction phases of the campus development process.

- A robust geodatabase forms the foundation for key applications that service reporting, project management, document management, and logistics and scheduling.

- ArcGIS for Server and ArcGIS for Windows Mobile make it easy for anyone with a web browser to check the status of the project visually in 2D, in 3D, or over time.

- Web-based sketching tools take a traditional pencil and paper process and make it digital for daily construction and logistics updates that can be shared, as appropriate, with all project team members.

- Through a mapping interface and dashboard, designers, planners, construction managers, project control managers, and other decision makers have ready access to information of all kinds, enabling better, more informed decisions.

Setting up a spatially enabled change process through the use of geodesign principles can save lots of time and money when used throughout a project's life cycle.

- Integrating key components of completed as-built drawings into a final geodatabase will form the foundation on which KU can build an enterprise system for the future management and growth of the KU system.

There is a saying in the GIS world that goes something like this: "Collect the data the right way the first time, and use it many times." That is what KU is doing now. The GIS data now being created for the Sabah Al-Salem University City—Kuwait University will form the foundational GIS on which the university can build and grow an enterprise GIS across the entire KU system to support operations, maintenance, and future redesign and expansion. At present there is no other university system in the region (and maybe the world?) that has such an integrated facility information management framework, thus the KU "eCampus" system could become a model to be emulated regionally and internationally.

It is the hope of the project managers that the enterprise GIS will be incorporated into an interdepartmental curriculum exploring ways to use geodesign to confront some of the world's most pressing problems in sustainability, resource use, and climate change. These ideas may include research methods, applications, and automated systems that have not even been invented yet that will help to usher in the high-tech knowledge-based economic vision of the region.

"Collect the data the right way the first time, and use it many times." That is what Kuwait University is doing now.

Key Links

Kuwait University
http://www.kuniv.edu/ku

OpenWare
http://www.openware.com.kw/

PenBay Solutions
http://www.penbaysolutions.com/

Turner Projacs (Joint Venture)
Turner Construction—http://www.turnerconstruction.com/
Projacs—http://www.projacs.com/

Acknowledgments

Thanks to Benton Yetman (director of strategic technology) and Ann Marie Lynch (marketing communications manager), both at PenBay Solutions, and Nishant Arora (project manager), Ahmed Muhisen (GIS consultant), and Ahmad Rasmi Mustafa (GIS consultant) at OpenWare, Kuwait. Additional thanks go to the director of the Kuwait University Construction Program (KUCP) Dr. Rana Al Fares, engineer Rana Majdalawieh (GIS coordinator) at Kuwait University, and Sammer Bushacra (project executive) and Maher El-Safarini (GIS coordinator) at Turner Projacs for their continued support.

Notes and References

[1] "Kuwait University," Wikipedia. Retrieved August 24, 2011, from http://en.wikipedia.org/wiki/Kuwait_University.

[2] "New University City in Shedadiya," Office of the Vice President for Planning, Kuwait University. Retrieved August 24, 2011, from http://www.planning.kuniv.edu.kw/English/ku%20new_city3.htm.

[3] "Projects," Kuwait University City web page, Happold Safe & Secure. Retrieved August 24, 2011, from http://www.happoldsafesecure.com/PROJ_KuwaitUniversityCity.aspx.

[4] "Kuwait University," Projects web page, WZMH Architects. Retrieved August 24, 2011, from http://www.wzmh.com/index.php/projects/institutional/kuwait_university/.

[5] LEED, or Leadership in Energy and Environmental Design, is an internationally recognized green building certification system developed by the US Green Building Council. LEED provides building owners and operators with a framework for identifying and implementing practical and measurable green building design, construction, operations, and maintenance solutions. Retrieved September 6, 2011, from http://www.usgbc.org/.

6 "Kuwait University," Projects web page, WZMH Architects. Retrieved August 24, 2011, from http://www.wzmh.com/index .php/projects/institutional/kuwait_university/.

7 "Balancing Act . . . Plans for Sustainable University Building in Kuwait's Challenging Climate Combine Community and Comfort with Low Energy Use," World Architecture News.com, February 26, 2010. Retrieved August 25, 2011, from http://www .worldarchitecturenews.com/index.php?fuseaction=wanappln .projectview&upload_id=13535.

8 "Kuwait—New University in Shedadiya," World Arab: Architecture, Art & Design. Retrieved August 24, 2011, from http://www.worldarab.net/ar/content /kuwait-new-university-city-shedadiya.

9 Carl Steinitz, GeoDesign Summit presentation, 2011.

10 Bill Miller, in discussion with the author, March 2011.

11 "Masdar City Master Plan Review Provides Progress Update," Masdar press release, October 10, 2010. Retrieved August 25, 2011, from http://www.masdar.ae/en/MediaArticle /NewsDescription.aspx?News_ID=150&News_Type=PR&MenuID =0&CatID=64.

7

Visioning Florida 2050

Florida and the Not Too Distant Future

The counties in east central Florida, historically, had one thing in common: oranges. Rolling hills covered with dark green foliage and the intoxicating scent of orange blossoms greeted visitors and locals alike. For 100 years and well into the 1970s, growers, packers, and processors were the backbone of the local economy. Today, most know the area for its cities, events, theme parks, and beaches. Names like Daytona and Orlando, Walt Disney World and Universal Studios Florida, not to mention a dozen other attractions, help make the area one of the most visited in the United States. Tourism has now become a mainstay of the east central Floridian economy.

Its attractions and tropical climate have also made it a prime place to live. Despite recent downturns, east central Florida is still projected to experience "explosive" growth over the next 50 years. If this growth follows historic trends, remaining agricultural land would be the first to go followed by the fragmentation or conversion of "virtually all the natural systems and wildlife corridors in this region."[1] The rural and natural character of Florida, its sense of place, would be threatened or lost.

With over 18 million residents today, Florida has already been challenged with the consequences of rampant sprawl, rapidly vanishing natural areas, and overcrowded roads.

Figure 7.1: Once the powerhouse of Florida's economy, orange groves are disappearing, replaced by residential and urban development. (Image copyright Jason Patrick Ross, 2011; used under license from Shutterstock.com)

Figure 7.2: Aerial view of the adventure park Sea World Orlando—one of the seven most-visited amusement parks in the United States in 2007. (Image copyright Nataliya Hora, 2011; used under license from Shutterstock.com)

"What will Florida look like in 2060, when its population is projected to reach almost 36 million?"[2] Is the answer more suburban sprawl, traffic congestion, and the loss of nature? True, divining the future may not be possible or even wise, but deciding what you value as a community and then devising a plan to move toward a better future are. And that is exactly what the East Central Florida Regional Planning Council (ECFRPC) did. Enlisting the help of Paul Zwick and Margaret Carr, director and codirector, respectively, of the GeoPlan Center at the University of Florida, it utilized geodesign principles, Esri ArcGIS, ArcGIS Spatial Analyst, and ModelBuilder to closely examine what the future might hold.

Got Sprawl?

How does sprawl, "the rapid and inefficient expansion of urban/suburban land use," happen?[3] First of all, it happens with the best of intentions driven by the housing needs of a burgeoning population, desire for larger homes at a lower cost, and governmental policies. Most of the time, it goes unnoticed until the unintended consequences of sprawl—the loss of wildlife, open space, and agricultural land, along with a marked increase in traffic congestion and pollution—begin to add up.

Who is to blame? Interestingly, nearly half of people asked this question blame builders, developers, and elected officials. Most people don't see themselves or their individual actions as the problem.[4] Part of the reason is that a single individual action by itself doesn't amount to much.

Most of the time, sprawl goes unnoticed until its unintended consequences—the loss of wildlife, open space, and agricultural land, along with a marked increase in traffic congestion and pollution—begin to add up.

It's the cumulative impact of everyone's actions that creates the problem. The rest of the reason is the incremental nature of land-use change. When land use changes one parcel at a time, it is difficult to see the change. But if all the changes that occur over a 10-year period are aggregated and then reviewed, the cumulative results are easy to see and

to examine the impact of alternative land-use allocations and development scenarios well into the future.

"Visualization and analysis of land use in major metropolitan urban areas that doesn't consider the larger regional context is ineffective. Regardless of one's philosophical view on urban/suburban expansion, the public will be best served when

Figure 7.3: Housing boomed over the last 20 years with sprawling suburbs that replaced both agricultural fields and wetlands. (Image copyright FloridaStock, 2011; used under license from Shutterstock.com)

understand. Yes, in this case, hindsight is 20/20. But what if there was a way to see the future, or at least a number of probable futures, ahead of time?[5]

That was the idea behind the creation of the Land Use Conflict Identification Strategy (LUCIS), a modeling technique created by the University of Florida that reveals the spatial reality of incremental land-use change and its impacts. LUCIS originally stopped just short of representing alternative futures, choosing to focus on the identification of conflict and bias among stakeholder groups.[6] But its latest incarnation, LUCIS Plus, goes quite a bit farther

the cumulative effect of land-use policies can be translated into comprehensible visualizations of the future; in other words, when what-if scenarios can be simplified to the point where they may be easily and satisfactorily understood" (Carr and Zwick 2007).

LUCIS Plus

Interestingly, LUCIS Plus in Latin means "more light," and perhaps that is an appropriate meaning for a modeling technique whose intention is to shed light on the problems associated with rapid development that, more often than not, concentrates on short-term gain and ignores the long-term ramifications. In actuality, LUCIS Plus is a goal-driven GIS modeling technique that allows stakeholders to visualize and assess the societal and environmental impacts of future land-use allocations. It utilizes suitability analyses to divide the landscape into a number of categories based on current, preferred, and probable land-use types as well as potential areas of conflict or opportunity. These "conflict and opportunity surfaces" (i.e., suitability map layers) are then used to develop alternative land-use change and development scenarios. Discussing and visualizing such scenarios help planners, landscape architects, politicians, and the public gain understanding and insight into the physical and social implications of projected future growth within a region.

LUCIS Plus, like geodesign, is a framework of processes and tools. Its conceptual basis was derived from the work of Eugene P. Odum (1913–2002), one of the twentieth century's foremost ecologists, who proposed a simplified compartmental model that combined *land-use types* and *ecosystem functions* to simulate human impact on the environment[7]—in essence, treating humans as part of nature, not separate from nature. Odum's model divided land use into four categories: productive, protective, compromise, and urban/industrial. To create greater contrast between land-use types, the LUCIS Plus model lumps these into three categories—agriculture, conservation, and urban. So how does LUCIS Plus work?

The LUCIS Plus model requires that three stakeholder groups are formed, one to represent each of the three land-use types. These groups serve as advocates for their specific category. Each group rates all lands in the study area for their relative suitability to support the land-use

category they represent "without regard for the motivations or preferences of the other groups." The role-playing approach tends to mimic the reality of the free market and helps to identify areas that will be in most conflict in the years to come.[8] This approach can also be used to identify mixed use or redevelopment opportunities between (1) retail, (2) commercial, and (3) multi-family residential within urban areas and across different development strategies.

The LUCIS Plus model includes a number of steps:

1. Develop goals and objectives (representative of community values).

2. Inventory available data relevant to each goal and objective (*representation models*).

3. Create criteria appropriate to define relative suitability for each goal/objective using experts (*process models*).

4. Create preferences using community values (*evaluation models*).

5. Combine preferences to identify areas of future land-use conflict or opportunity for mixed-use development (*evaluation models*).

6. Develop future land-use allocation and growth scenarios based on community values defined in step 1 (*change models*).

7. Compare the impact on key performance indicators of each future growth scenario using the current growth trend as a base (*impact models*).

8. Pick the preferred future growth scenario (*decision models*).

"The public will be best served when the cumulative effect of land-use policies can be translated into comprehensible visualizations of the future…"

Margaret H. Carr and Paul D. Zwick, *Smart Land-Use Analysis*

LUCIS Plus is a goal-driven GIS modeling technique that allows stakeholders to visualize and assess the societal and environmental impacts of future land-use allocations.

During these mapping events, participants placed dots on areas where they wished to see development in the coming years.

East Central Florida Visioning Process

So how did this work in east central Florida? The ECFRPC started with a visioning effort that involved 20,000 people across seven counties who participated in 150 public meetings, 30 of which involved active participation in "Development Dot" mapping games (figure 7.4). During these mapping events, participants placed dots on areas where they wished to see development in the coming years. Interestingly, most participants declined to draw any new roads, favoring to draw public transit routes instead. Three major themes or values emerged from these workshops that would end up defining future development scenarios:

- Centers—To concentrate development around urban cores

- Corridors—To establish high-density urban corridors

- Conservation—To conserve green space

These themes showed a clear preference for the retention of green space, the preservation of conservation areas, and the redevelopment of current urban centers, a marked change from the historic and current regional pattern of low-density sprawl. The end result of such a shift in development patterns would be the preservation of sensitive ecosystems and migratory animal corridors, the redevelopment and strengthening of current urban centers, and the preservation of the rural and natural look and feel of the Floridian landscape.

To demonstrate the differences between these value-based themes required the modeling of four alternative future growth scenarios—*Trend, Conservation, Centers,* and *Corridors*—comparing each alternative to a series of key performance indicators:

- Total additional area urbanized (square miles)

- Additional habitat destroyed (square miles)

- Green areas added (square miles)

- Auto commute time (minutes per person per day)

- Average auto speed (mph)

- Total passenger rail + streetcar (miles of track)

- Air quality (millions of kilograms of carbon)

- Water consumed (1.56 billion gallons per day)

- Employment (trend + the new amount)

- Economy (in 2000 dollars) (trend + the new amount)

- Average annual wage (in 2007 dollars)

Population, land-use allocation, traffic, and the economic impacts of each growth scenario were modeled out to 2050 based on government and industry projections.[9] In all four resulting scenario maps, gray represents urban area in 2005, yellow represents urbanized area 2005–2050, and dark green represents conservation land.

Figure 7.4: Development Dots mapped for intensity show red areas as most intense, yellow as least, and green as green space. (Courtesy of ECFRPC and University of Florida)

To demonstrate the differences between these value-based themes required the modeling of four alternative future growth scenarios—*Trend*, *Conservation*, *Centers*, and *Corridors*—comparing each alternative to a series of key performance indicators.

In all four scenario maps, gray represents urban area in 2005, yellow represents urbanized area 2005–2050, and various shades of green represent conservation land 2005–2050.

The Trend 2050 Scenario

Continued current development patterns and low population densities would double the amount of developed land, allowing low-density residential sprawl to convert remaining agricultural lands and critical ecosystems into urban areas. City boundaries would meld together with little distinction.

Outcomes

- Urbanizes an additional 2,577 square miles of land by 2050

- Estimated infrastructure cost of $148 billion

- Destroys 344 square miles of habitat

- Makes major population shifts into Polk, Lake, and Volusia Counties

Figure 7.5: Trend 2050 scenario. Gray signifies current urban areas in 2005. Notice how much would be converted to urban (yellow) by 2050. (Courtesy of ECFRPC and University of Florida)

The Green Areas 2050 (conservation) Scenario

This scenario emphasized protecting and connecting natural ecosystems throughout the region and provided additional open space where 3,000 workshop attendees placed green dots signifying areas they would like to see conserved.

Outcomes

- Urbanizes an additional 918 square miles of land by 2050

- Estimated infrastructure cost of $53 billion

- Destroys 45 square miles of habitat (209 square miles less than the Trend)

- Makes major population shifts into Polk and Lake Counties

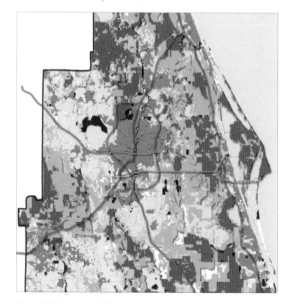

Figure 7.6: Green Areas 2050 scenario. Notice the growth in green areas and a reduction in yellow "future" urban growth areas. (Courtesy of ECFRPC and University of Florida)

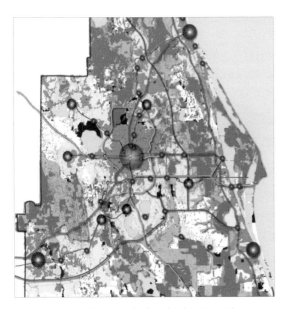

Figure 7.7: Centers 2050 scenario. Graduated circles using a violet to purple to blue color ramp mark the location and intensity of city center development. (Courtesy of ECFRPC and University of Florida)

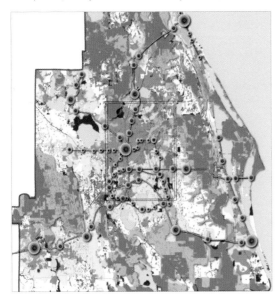

Figure 7.8: Corridors 2050 scenario. Graduated circles using a bull's-eye symbol signify distributed urban development along corridors. (Courtesy of ECFRPC and University of Florida)

The Centers 2050 Scenario

This scenario emphasized promoting more growth in existing urban centers, keeping critical ecosystem corridors connected while adding some rail transit.

Outcomes

- Urbanizes an additional 844 square miles of land by 2050

- Estimated infrastructure cost of $49 billion

- Destroys 45 square miles of habitat (209 square miles less than the Trend)

- Adds 370 miles of new toll roads, 282 miles of rail transit

- Opens up sensitive habitat to urban development

The Corridors 2050 Scenario

This scenario allocated population along high-density mixed-use rail corridors. It only adds one person per urban acre for an average urban density of 3.15 persons per acre.

Outcomes

- Urbanizes an additional 660 square miles of land by 2050

- Estimated infrastructure cost of $38 billion

- Destroys 28 square miles of habitat (316 square miles less than the Trend)

- Adds 413 miles of rail transit, with major intensity increases around rail stops

- Saves $110 billion in unnecessary infrastructure over the Trend

Public involvement at key decision points was critical to defining a "consensus vision" that met the needs of both the people and the environment.

Ranking the Four Choices

Once the models had been run to show the impact of the four model types, additional input was needed to determine which alternative scenario would be the most favored choice. So in January 2007, a one-hour public television program was aired in prime time for five consecutive nights on station WMFE to educate the public about regional growth issues and enlist them in the debate.

After the final night of television coverage, the audience was asked to visit the Internet website to select their preferences from the four alternative future growth scenarios. They were also asked to choose which key indicators they would prefer for their region. Within two weeks' time, 7,319 people visited the website and selected their preferences for the scenarios and for a series of the following indicators:

- Percentage of Developed Land, 2050

- Percentage of Conserved Land, 2050

- Air Quality, 2050

- Water Demand, 2050

- Transportation Choices, 2050

- Commute Times, 2050

- Economic Impact, 2050

Two results were obvious from the Internet surveys. First, 96 percent rejected the Trend scenario as their first choice. Second, none of the scenarios garnered more than 50 percent of the votes. The indicators survey clearly showed that a combination of the Corridors scenario, with the best points from Centers and Conservation, seemed to be the consensus vision for future growth:

- Develop the least amount of land (Corridors)

- Conserve the most natural resources (Green Areas)

- Attain the best air quality (Centers)

- Reduce water demand (Corridors)

- Provide the most transportation choices (Corridors)

- Have the shortest commute time (Centers)

- Stimulate the most robust economy (Corridors)

This consensus vision became the "4Cs" regional vision:[10]

- Conserve the most critical natural resources, and do this first.

- Promote more growth in walkable, great urban centers, with amenities such as parks, live-and-work neighborhoods, and cultural and educational centers all in close proximity.

- Connect major centers with corridors served by a balanced multimodal transportation system of roads, rail transit (commuter rail, light rail, and streetcar), bus rapid transit, buses, and bike and pedestrian ways.

- Take the pressure off countryside, so viable agriculture and open land are still abundant.

Regional Growth Vision 2050

Map Area

Map Key

- Hamlet: Less than 4,999
- Village: 5,000-9,999
- Town: 10,000-29,999
- Small City: 30,000-49,999
- Medium City: 50,000-99,999
- Regional City: 100,000 or more

- Undeveloped Area (2050)
- Suggested Conservation/Countryside (2050)
- Existing Conservation (2006)
- Major Water Bodies
- Developed Area (2005)

- Active Railroad
- Inactive Railroad
- Highway
- Conceptual Multi-Modal Regional Transportation Connections (2050)

- Kennedy Space Center
- International Airport
- International Port

Figure 7.9: Artist rendering of the regional vision. Centers are shown with 3D blocks that signify population density connected by conceptual transportation ribbons. (Courtesy of ECFRPC and University of Florida)

The 2050 Regional Growth Vision was unanimously endorsed and adopted by the East Central Florida Regional Planning Council and all 93 central Florida land-use jurisdictions.

The 4Cs (conservation, centers, corridors, and countryside) 2050 Regional Growth Vision was unanimously endorsed and adopted by the East Central Florida Regional Planning Council, myregion.org, and representatives of all 93 central Florida land-use jurisdictions.

Following the completion of the regional visioning process in August 2007, the ECFRPC

CHAPTER 11: AGRICULTURE	
Goal	Promote a regional agricultural system that results in gains to the local economy, greater food security, preservation of rural heritage, and improved land stewardship and agricultural practices.
Policy 11.1	Protect and conserve lands for long-term agricultural use.
Policy 11.2	Promote agriculture as a viable land use and protect farming operations from incompatible adjacent land uses.
Policy 11.3	Conserve and promote the integrity of the region's rural character.
Policy 11.4	Encourage best management agricultural practices that reduce impacts to the function and value of natural systems.

Figure 7.10: The real benefits of the process became evident when policy statements were written into the overall visioning plan that captured core values defined by the whole that seek to maximize benefit to their environment and well-being without threat to their economy, as exemplified in this snippet of their agriculture goals and policies. (Courtesy of ECFRPC and University of Florida)

Transparency, openness, and trust were established, all key to successful adoption.

staff began the work of reviewing the 1998 Policy Plan and initiating research into current conditions and policy directions for the updated Strategic Regional Policy Plan.

Discussion

The LUCIS Plus model as it is used in this case is a good example of the geodesign framework being utilized at a regional, county, and city scale to help drive wise land-use decisions. It started

as a regional visioning effort, but ultimately, it brought people together to discuss the future by examining the impact of alternative scenarios.

The LUCIS Plus model closely tracks with Steinitz's six-step geodesign framework, starting with stakeholder involvement to define broad values that are then refined into clear statements of intent supported by goals with corresponding objectives. The importance of this step to the whole process was considerable in that it ensured that people were heard, issues were identified, and options were discussed among everyone. Transparency, openness, and trust were established, all key to successful adoption.

Clear goal and objective statements also drove the data inventory and process modeling steps of the geodesign process itself. For example, the statement of intent for agriculture—identify lands most suitable for agricultural use—required the definition of agriculture land categories (e.g., croplands, livestock, orchards, timber). These categories then required the identification of physical and economic suitability criteria. For example, cropland required relatively flat land with good soil that is in close proximity to a market for that crop that commands an economically viable market price. *Representation models* and *process models* thus had to cover geology, soils, hydrology, demographics, transportation, built environment, and current land use, among others.

The next step was to use the suitability criteria to create suitability models of various complexities (*evaluation models*). This was accomplished using ArcGIS ModelBuilder. With a visual model, it was easy to see the big picture, an entire methodology, laid out in a logical pattern that graphically reinforced the concepts behind the analysis. It took some effort to build, but once built, it was easily altered; perfect for such a large, complex, regional design effort as this one that required numerous small adjustments to parts of the project as it grew.

Once suitability models had been established and the models run, it was time to determine preference. Instead of asking the question, "Which land use is most suitable?" the question was asked, "Which land use is most important?" This again required involving stakeholders who were asked to weight the level of importance of each land-use type on a scale of 1 to 9. The resulting

preference maps were then combined to identify future areas of conflict among land-use types, but they also identified areas open to possible mixed land-use strategies. For example, an area that is both a 9 for conservation and a 9 for urban are clear areas of conflict, whereas an area that has a 3 for agriculture, a 3 for conservation, and a 3 for urban might be open to a combination of complementary design program elements. These weighted map layers would inform the creation and placement of the alternative development scenarios.

The possible future development strategies of centers, corridors, and green areas (*change models*) went through a very similar model development strategy, but rather than focus on conflict and opportunity, this stage focused on the development of key performance indicators that measured the environmental and economic impacts related to changes in urban form and transportation (*impact models*). Not surprisingly, the three alternatives all fared better when compared to the trend of continued sprawl, with the Corridors scenario having the overall best numbers per indicator.

The decision-making process (*decision models*) was quite unique in terms of its magnitude and staging. The first was the attempt at inclusion across jurisdictions (seven counties) and people. Reaching out to 20,000 people at the start of the effort helped educate them on the issues, define the issues, and ultimately create important stakeholder buy-in. Opening the door at various stages to allow stakeholders to participate in the weighting or preference of land-use types was another.

And finally, the opening of the entire conversation to the public through public access television, and a web-based voting process to

Instead of asking the question, "Which land use is most suitable?" the question was asked, "Which land use is most important?"

The LUCIS Plus modeling technique helps turn ad hoc development into better planning by clearly revealing the true impact of incremental land-use change over time.

allow participants to select preferred development scenarios and key performance indicators, built further consensus on key areas of agreement. The participants completely rejected the trend (by 96%), favoring the other three alternative scenarios fairly evenly.

Lessons Learned

Spatial decision support tools like LUCIS Plus can be very effective in managing the complexity of local and regional planning activities. Some of the lessons learned include the following:

- Regional urban form can be determined based on informed decisions that are generated from GIS models.

- Regional geodesign models can produce results that are summarized to local areas, making regional planning proactive, flexible, and community based.

- Regional geodesign/planning will be less unpredictable and ultimately produce fewer unintended consequences.

- Existing land-use plans can be compared to multiple geodesign alternatives, producing plans that are based on truly informed policy decisions.

- Policy alternatives can be tested and refined to produce a more sustainable urban form without interfering with design creativity.

- Planners and urban designers can function within an environment based on identified parameters and still allow designers freedom within site design.

- Design impacts can be tested within local or regional areas and more easily explained to the general public.

- Regional geodesign criteria can guide site design by specifying parameters that support regional policy with minimal design interference.

As in any participatory planning effort, the process can be as important as the technology. Success relies on remembering these three rules:

Work collaboratively—Those who have lived through a hurricane or helped pick up the pieces after one has passed know firsthand that weather systems are not confined by any jurisdictional boundaries. The same goes for the cumulative impact of land-use changes. The decision of one city or county can cause radical change to its neighbors. Effective land-use change must consider the larger regional impacts in the near term and, maybe even more importantly, the long term. The implementation of a regional vision plan can only be achieved by working collaboratively and across jurisdictional boundaries.

Allow for creativity—How a community chooses to implement a given plan is ultimately up to it. That said, the policies derived from such planning efforts as this should foster creativity and unconventional thought processes. Communities should not prescribe a rigid rule structure that can become outdated or otherwise hamper truly imaginative concepts.

Be flexible—Planning for truly great places and communities requires active citizen engagement absent of political agendas, bureaucratic rule making, and archaic institutional controls.

Urban planners, elected officials, and others who make land-use decisions face tough choices that are hard to conceptualize, much less communicate to the public and other stakeholders. The LUCIS Plus modeling technique helps turn ad hoc development into better planning by clearly revealing the true impact of incremental land-use change over time. Through community collaboration, creativity, and careful consideration of the long-term impacts of our choices, we can design a better world.

Key Links

University of Florida, GeoPlan Center
http://www.geoplan.ufl.edu/

Smart Land-Use Analysis—The LUCIS Model
esripress.esri.com/display/index.cfm?fuseaction=display
&websiteID=115&moduleID=0

myregion.org
http://www.myregion.org/

East Central Florida 2060
http://www.ecfrpc.org/Document-Library/SRPP/East-Central
-Florida-2060-Plan.aspx

East Central Florida Regional Planning Council
http://www.ecfrpc.org/Home.aspx

Acknowledgments

Thanks go to Paul Zwick, director, and Margaret Carr, codirector, of the GeoPlan Center at the University of Florida for contributing content. Thanks also go to the project's sponsor, the East Central Florida Regional Planning Council.

Notes and References

[1] 1000 Friends of Florida, *Florida in 2060: Not a Pretty Picture? An Executive Summary*, December 2006. Retrieved September 1, 2011, from http://www.1000friendsofflorida.org /PUBS/2060/2060-executive-summary-Final.pdf.

[2] Ibid.

[3] Margaret H. Carr and Paul D. Zwick, *Smart Land-Use Analysis* (Redlands, CA: Esri Press, 2007), 4.

[4] National Association of Realtors (NAR) and National Association of Home Builders (NAHB), "Consumers' Survey on Smart Choices for Home Buyers," April 2002.

[5] Carr and Zwick, *Smart Land-Use Analysis*, 5.

[6] Margaret H. Carr and Paul Zwick, "Using GIS Suitability Analysis to Identify Potential Future Land Use Conflicts in North Central Florida," *Journal of Conservation Planning* 1 (2005): 58–73.

[7] Eugene P. Odum, "The Strategy of Ecosystem Development," *Science* 164 (1969): 262–70.

[8] Carr and Zwick, *Smart Land-Use Analysis*, 11–13.

[9] East Central Florida Regional Planning Council, "The State of the Region," chap. 1 in *East Central Florida 2060 Plan*, December 29, 2009. Retrieved September 21, 2011, from http:// www.ecfrpc.org/Document-Library/SRPP/East-Central-Florida -2060-Plan.aspx.

[10] "Four Themes (4C's)," myregion.org regional vision web page. Retrieved October 3, 2011, from http://www.myregion .org/index.php?submenu=FourThemes&src=gendocs&ref =FourThemes4Cs&category=RegionalVision.

8

Red Fields into Green Fields

"Tearing down can create wealth. Land without buildings should be considered an asset by our financial system."

Michael Messner

It's All Connected

Geodesign is about holistic design and communication. It is about easily linking seemingly disparate data into a cohesive graphic language that can tell a story far more powerfully than its individual parts. Nowhere is this better illustrated than in the story of how something as humble and democratic as a park could help reverse the country's economic malaise caused by bad loans, foreclosures, and vacant lots while addressing social inequity, public health, and pollution.

Michael Messner, a Wall Street fund manager and cofounder of the Speedwell Foundation, proposed Red Fields to Green Fields (R2G), a plan for turning distressed properties (red fields) into parks (green fields). His argument is simple—remove the glut of overbuilt and foreclosed properties and redeploy that capital out of under-performing real estate and into green space.[1] It would stabilize property values, strengthen banks, and create jobs. As Messner puts it, "Tearing down can create wealth. Land without buildings should be considered an asset by our financial system."[2] He goes on to point out that the benefits are far more than financial.

In essence, parks benefit the "triple bottom line" by improving economic, social, and environmental health of communities. From New York City's Central Park to the city of Boulder, Colorado's greenbelt, history has shown that parks and open space tend to increase nearby property values; attract tourists and residents who contribute to local commerce; increase public health by providing opportunities for physical recreation and mental relaxation; and perform vital environmental services such as treating storm water, reducing heat island effect, and improving air quality.

Los Angeles was one of 11 cities selected to test the viability of the R2G concept. The Red Fields to Green Fields Los Angeles (R2G-LA) case study was developed by the Verde Coalition with the help of several agencies including the Trust for Public Land, Occidental College's Urban and Environmental Policy Institute, Parks for People, and Cal Poly Pomona's Landscape Architecture Department 606 Studio. The 606 Studio played a significant role in developing the R2G-LA case, utilizing a geodesign workflow and a combination of Esri ArcGIS, CAD, Google SketchUp, and Adobe Illustrator and Photoshop to assist in the inventory, analysis, selection, and conceptual design of key parks in the city of Los Angeles.

City of Angels—Defining the Issues

Nicknamed the "City of Angels," Los Angeles is an economic powerhouse ranked as the third-richest and fifth most powerful and influential city in the world. It is also recognized as the most

Figure 8.1: A vision of red to green field transformation. (From Dakotah Bertsch, Michael Boucher, Eran James, and Abby Jones, *Red Fields to Green Fields Los Angeles*, Pomona: California Polytechnic University 606 Studio; used by permission)

Lack of parks is not the only disparity. Food deserts, obesity, asthma, and other ailments associated with lack of open space and low income dominate in these areas.

diverse metropolitan area in the United States. However, compared to other large cities within the United States, Los Angeles's parkland falls short in terms of both its percentage of the city's land area and acres per resident.[3] While a few large tracts of parkland do exist, parks are not distributed equally throughout the city, being especially deficient in lower income neighborhoods typically dominated by people of color.[4] In Los Angeles, predominantly white neighborhoods enjoy 31.8 acres of park space for every 1,000 people, compared with 1.7 acres in African-American neighborhoods and 0.6 acres in Latino neighborhoods.[5]

The first step in a geodesign project typically starts by examining the geographic context of the area of interest to identify key issues that will help define goals.

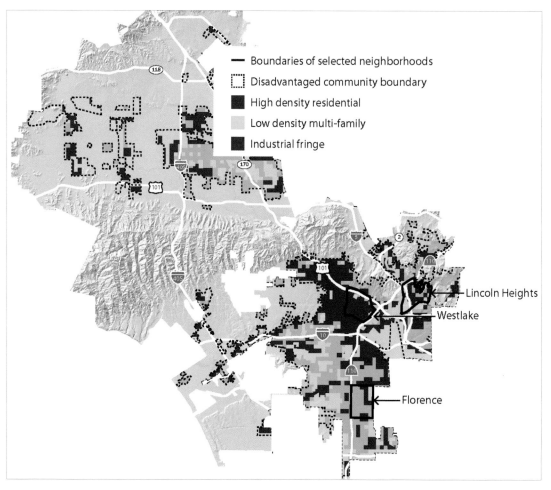

Figure 8.2: ArcMap, 2000 Census data, and land-use data from both Esri and the Southern California Association of Governments (SCAG) were used to identify three areas that were both park-poor and economically disadvantaged (outlined in black). (From Dakotah Bertsch, Michael Boucher, Eran James, and Abby Jones, *Red Fields to Green Fields Los Angeles*, Pomona: California Polytechnic University 606 Studio; used by permission)

Lack of parks is not the only disparity. Food deserts, obesity, asthma, and other ailments associated with lack of open space and low income dominate in these areas. Poor environmental quality is also highest in these communities.[6] During the recession, property values plummeted everywhere, but disadvantaged communities were hit hardest. Home values in portions of the San Fernando Valley dropped 44 percent, South Los Angeles 62 percent, Westlake 41 percent, and Lincoln Heights 41 percent, more than twice the rate of affluent West Los Angeles, which dropped 20 percent.[7]

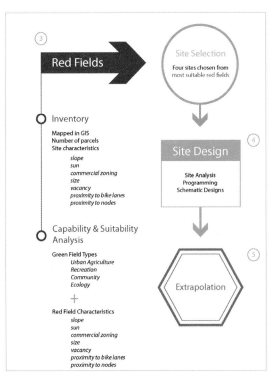

Figure 8.3: The R2G-LA method diagram outlines the design workflow in terms of scale, complexity, and detail needed for each stage. In this case, extrapolation is synonymous with calculation of the potential cumulative impact that a fully implemented R2G-LA program might have. (From Dakotah Bertsch, Michael Boucher, Eran James, and Abby Jones, *Red Fields to Green Fields Los Angeles*, Pomona: California Polytechnic University 606 Studio; used by permission)

Geodesign is about discovery. It is investigative. It is about reading the landscape to tease out what is most important.

Defining Area of Need

The first step in a geodesign project typically starts by examining the geographic context of the area of interest to identify key issues that will help define goals. Given the context described above, the R2G-LA goals were to improve environmental, social, and economic health by converting distressed properties to open space starting in areas of highest need. The first step—identify the most park-poor and economically disadvantaged neighborhoods in Los Angeles. A park-poor area was defined as having three acres or less of parkland per 1,000 people based on census tract data. An economically disadvantaged area was defined as census tracts with a median household income that is 80 percent of the state median household income. These two criteria were based on California Proposition 84 funding standards, which have been instrumental in providing funding for parks and nature facilities in California, a good example of how *value-based* policy decisions can influence a geodesign effort. At the regional scale, these two criteria formed the basis of the geodesign *evaluation models* that would result in the identification of three neighborhoods that best demonstrated the urban characteris-

As is the case with large, complex design projects like this one, the investigation started at a regional level and worked its way down to the parcel.

ArcGIS played a significant role by providing the data storage framework necessary to store, analyze, query, and visualize economic, environmental, and social data across multiple scales.

tics typified in areas of need: Lincoln Heights, Westlake, and Florence (figure 8.2).

Working across Scales

Geodesign is about discovery. It is investigative. It is about reading the landscape to tease out what is most important. Since it is holistic in nature, it requires gathering diverse geographic data covering the natural, cultural, and built environments. As is the case with large, complex design projects like this one, the investigation started at a regional level and worked its way down to the parcel. ArcGIS played a significant role by providing the data storage framework necessary to store, analyze, query, and visualize economic, environmental, and social data across multiple scales.

Data inventories had to be collected and/or created for each level of investigation to meet the informational demands of each scale, from regional to neighborhood to the site (*representation models*). Existing data, along with data collected from site visits, was used to illustrate how the site was working (*process models*) and if the site was working well (*evaluation models*).

A combination of GIS data and on-the-ground site investigations and analyses helped the 606 Studio design team select appropriate design program elements crucial to the creation of preliminary and conceptual design drawings (*change models*) that would turn red fields into green fields, given site constraints and community need.

A key feature of geodesign in practice is the quantification of a design's impacts. In this case, the final step was the extrapolation of impacts from a single site back up to the region to show the cumulative benefits that would result from the transformation of numerous site-scale red fields to

Figure 8.4: Red field in Lincoln Heights, Los Angeles. (From Dakotah Bertsch, Michael Boucher, Eran James, and Abby Jones, *Red Fields to Green Fields Los Angeles*, Pomona: California Polytechnic University 606 Studio; used by permission)

green fields throughout the city (*impact models*). The results of this analysis are being used to help government officials and other stakeholders build support to fund some of the proposed R2G-LA strategies (*decision models*).

Red Fields

Red fields are parcels of land that, for various reasons, are not functioning at their highest civic capacity. Many are vacant lots, brownfields, or foreclosed properties and contain run-down or collapsing buildings. Commercial real estate data helped narrow the search down to individual parcels; however, early site investigation showed many vacant lots and distressed properties to be missing from the data. The 606 Studio team surveyed all three neighborhoods to locate, ground truth, and inventory site characteristics for all available red fields. The site inventories provided a much more in-depth understanding of red field conditions and their community context, invaluable for later site design. The total number of red fields found in all the neighborhoods was 138 sites, with a total area of 67 acres.

The inventory included relative sun exposure; size; commercial use or zoning; average slope; buildings present; land-use designation; ownership; and proximity to the network of planned bike lanes, Metro stations, and major commercial intersections (nodes), which are indicative of higher than normal pedestrian use.

Green Fields

Green field types were developed that address the social, environmental, and economic needs of Los Angeles communities. The four broad categories of green field types were *urban agriculture, recreation, community,* and *ecology.* Urban agriculture green field solutions support food production in the context of the urban environment through community gardening, farming, composting, or production of value-added products from agriculture. Recreation green field solutions refer to parks, sports fields, trails, or other facilities that promote active or passive physical activity. Community green field solutions focus on building community capital through social, cultural, educational, or artistic exchanges by creating plazas or space for community interaction. Ecology green field solutions provide ecological function and opportunities for people to connect with nature, for example, through engineered wetlands or reintroduction of native vegetation. The question was how to determine which green field solution was best for which red field site.

Capability Analysis

One of the great advantages of GIS is the ability to process, sift through, and visualize large amounts of data. With 138 red field sites, four green field types, and numerous criteria identifying which sites were capable of supporting a particular green field solution, the creation of capability models (a type of *evaluation model*) became the first task.

The primary characteristics used to define the capability criteria for green field types were slope, sun, and commercial zoning. Different combinations of criteria were selected for each green field type (urban agriculture, recreation, community, and ecology). For example, sites deemed capable for urban agriculture had to be sunny with slopes of less than 15 percent. Lack of sun is a limitation for most food crops, and steep slopes could increase risk of erosion, cause access issues, or

One of the great advantages of GIS is the ability to process, sift through, and visualize large amounts of data.

Figure 8.5: Lincoln Heights red fields capable of (1) agriculture, (2) community, (3) recreation, and (4) ecology. (From Dakotah Bertsch, Michael Boucher, Eran James, and Abby Jones, *Red Fields to Green Fields Los Angeles*, Pomona: California Polytechnic University 606 Studio; used by permission)

The site selection process was based on identifying neighborhoods of highest need and then narrowing that down to individual parcels using a suitability analysis.

require cost-prohibitive terracing. For the recreation green field type, having a gentle slope was the only criterion.

A GIS model was created using these capability requirements to identify red fields that met the criteria for each category. Maps were then created to show only those red fields capable for each green field type. The visualization of this data as 2D map layouts helped project participants understand what types of green field solutions were possible at any given site.

Because some sites were found to be capable of supporting multiple green field types, a "bar chart" map was created to allow side-by-side comparison (see figure 8.6).

Suitability Analysis

Because most red fields were capable of supporting several green field types, suitability modeling (*evaluation model*) was conducted to help determine which sites would be the "most suitable" for a particular green field development. This was done by examining criteria related to size; vacancy; and proximity to bike lanes, Metro stations (nodes), and major commercial intersections (nodes). The results of the suitability modeling were more selective than those that were obtained with capability mapping alone.

Suitability criteria were equally weighted but

determined to be cumulative, so that sites that met multiple criteria would have a higher level of suitability than sites that only met one criterion.

Suitability maps were made to show suitable red fields for each major green field type. The size of circles on these maps is representative of the number of suitability criteria met by a given red field; the larger the circle, the higher the suitability.

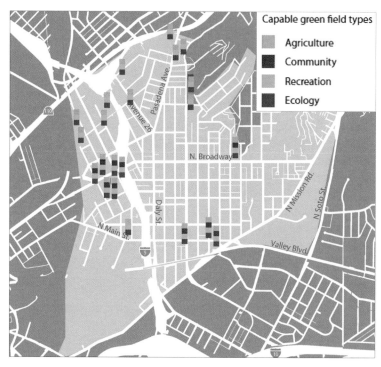

Figure 8.6: Lincoln Heights aggregated capability bar chart map. (From Dakotah Bertsch, Michael Boucher, Eran James, and Abby Jones, *Red Fields to Green Fields Los Angeles*, Pomona: California Polytechnic University 606 Studio; used by permission)

Following the suitability mapping, red fields with the highest two levels of suitability for each green field type were isolated and combined into one bar chart map for each neighborhood.

Suitability bar chart maps were again used

Figure 8.7: Lincoln Heights Local site location. (From Dakotah Bertsch, Michael Boucher, Eran James, and Abby Jones, *Red Fields to Green Fields Los Angeles*, Pomona: California Polytechnic University 606 Studio; used by permission)

Once a site has been selected, a detailed opportunities and constraints analysis of the site must be performed.

to allow simultaneous comparison of the distribution of red fields that were most suited to each green field type. Comparison of capability maps with suitability maps revealed that the number of suitable red field sites had been reduced through this process of refinement. When sites were later selected for example site designs, they were chosen from among these most suitable red fields.

Site Selection—One of Many Decision Points

Defining how decisions are going to be made, the *decision model* is at least as important, if not more important, than any other part of the geodesign process. One of those decision points was the selection of sites for design. The site selection process was based on identifying neighborhoods of highest need and then narrowing that down to individual parcels using a suitability analysis. One highly suitable site for each green field type was chosen from the list of suitable sites. The result was four red field sites representing a broad range of conditions

and uses. Two sites were chosen from Lincoln Heights, one from Westlake, and one from Florence.

Due to case study length limitations, example maps and images have targeted the Lincoln Heights Local red field site (see figure 8.7). For the rest of this case study, Lincoln Heights Local will be used for the green field site development discussion.

Lincoln Heights Local Site Analysis

Once a site has been selected, a detailed opportunities and constraints analysis of the site must be performed. For conceptual design, this required walking the site and making keen observations that would be used to define program elements for various possible designs. These are collected as photographs, narratives, site sketches, and maps.

This larger red field is a sloped, vacant lot located on Broadway, a busy commercial street in one of the oldest neighborhoods of Los Angeles. Multiple schools surround the site, including a high school, elementary school, preschool, and

This site would focus on promoting healthy food options and building community.

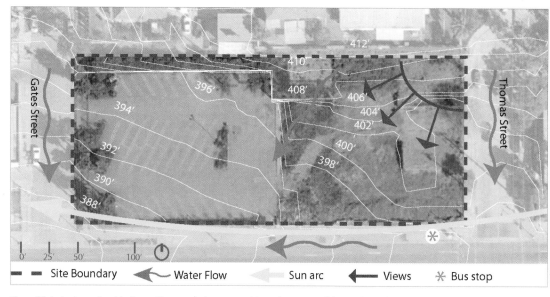

Figure 8.8: A simple map/graphic diagram illustrates the key opportunities and constraints of the Lincoln Heights Local site analysis. Arrows represent direction of sun movement, water flow, or views. The map shows just enough detail to support the development of various design program elements. (From Dakotah Bertsch, Michael Boucher, Eran James, and Abby Jones, *Red Fields to Green Fields Los Angeles*, Pomona: California Polytechnic University 606 Studio; used by permission)

kindergarten. An adjacent bus stop on Broadway is heavily used by high school students and other residents.

The site has steep topography on one side, providing views of buildings in downtown Los Angeles, and a relatively flat parking lot on the other side. It has high visibility, good accessibility, and a stream of pedestrians passing by—particularly at the beginning and end of the school day. The south-facing site receives full sunlight. A short list of constraints and opportunities included the following:

- Site area: 1.1 acres

- Neighborhood density: 10,602 people/ square mile

- Surrounding uses: Schools, residential, commercial

- Adjacent bus stop

- Sloped topography with views of city

- Pedestrian traffic from high school

- Good visibility, accessibility, and parking

- Must handle water drainage

- Might need terracing

Program Development

The site's suitability for *urban agriculture* and *community green field* types presented the opportunity to identify programming that would demonstrate the positive relationships to be had by combining these two types. A community garden

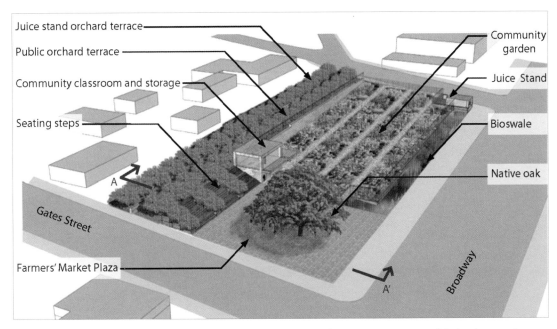

Juice stand orchard terrace

Public orchard terrace

Community classroom and storage

Seating steps

Gates Street

Farmers' Market Plaza

Community garden

Juice Stand

Bioswale

Native oak

Broadway

A

A'

Figure 8.9: Bird's-eye view of the Lincoln Heights Local design provides a perspective view along one axis giving a more realistic view of program elements. (From Dakotah Bertsch, Michael Boucher, Eran James, and Abby Jones, *Red Fields to Green Fields Los Angeles*, Pomona: California Polytechnic University 606 Studio; used by permission)

and a farmers' market plaza, representing urban agriculture and community green field types, respectively, were the best fit, both programmatically and physically, given the opportunities and constraints of the site.

This site would focus on promoting healthy food options and building community. The community garden would provide plots to surrounding schools as well as other members of the community. There students could grow their own food while learning about natural processes. The top floor of the community building would serve as an indoor classroom, while the bottom floor would house garden tools.

The farmers' market plaza, with a large oak tree, would host weekly farmers' markets as well as other community events such as health fairs, arts and crafts

fairs, and flea markets. The juice stand would utilize fruit from the on-site orchard as well as other fresh produce that would provide healthy snack alternatives to the high school and neighborhood.

Benefits

Built-in seating would enhance the functionality of the plaza and provide people with the option of dining on-site after purchasing healthy food at the farmers' market or juice stand or meeting with friends. Focusing on the local needs of the people while taking care of the environment provides numerous benefits to the community:

- Hands-on agriculture provides agricultural education and healthy food for schoolchildren.

Photorealistic renderings backed by GIS analyses and hard data help community members, government officials, and special interest groups understand the consequences of a particular design so they can make better, more informed decisions.

Figure 8.10: The photorealistic design rendering was produced using a combination of CAD, SketchUp, and Photoshop. (From Dakotah Bertsch, Michael Boucher, Eran James, and Abby Jones, *Red Fields to Green Fields Los Angeles*, Pomona: California Polytechnic University 606 Studio; used by permission)

- Farmers' market provides fresh produce and local economic exchange.

- Juice stand with neighborhood bulletin board informs the neighborhood about healthy food options.

- Oak and citrus trees on-site sequester carbon, reduce the heat island effect, and improve air quality.

- Bioswale cleans runoff.

Site Design

Design renderings were produced to better illustrate the design concepts that had been developed for each site. Care was taken to ensure that the designs were appropriate applications of green field solutions to the specific site conditions, as well as to the neighborhood context and regional objectives. Photorealistic renderings backed by GIS analyses and hard data help community members, government officials, and special interest groups understand the consequences of a particular design so they can make better, more informed decisions.

The Big Picture

At the start of the project, the 606 Studio design team used GIS to identify area of need, moving from the regional scale down to individual neighborhoods to identify a broad spectrum of sites appropriate for green field development. It was now time to look at the big picture, the cumulative impact of a red field to green field initiative that encompassed all sites within the city of Los Angeles *area of need*. To answer that question, the team used the ground-truthed red field inventory data as proxies to extrapolate the data back up to a regional scale.

If all the *area of need's* red fields were converted to green fields, park space would more than double in the disadvantaged communities of Los Angeles. It is estimated that a $7.2 billion investment would allow Los Angeles to rebuild disadvantaged neighborhoods, add vital park space, and improve economic conditions citywide. Converting red fields to green fields would reduce disparities between communities and strengthen the city's social, economic, and environmental health. It would remove underperforming and distressed properties from the market and bank ledgers and fund existing park projects and new green infrastructure, including the much-needed rehabilitation of the Los Angeles River. The resulting network of green fields would help unite the city's rich multicultural resources and help achieve the mayor's goal of making Los Angeles one of the greenest cities in the nation.[8] Here are some of the key impacts the R2G-LA effort could have:

- Create 77,000 new jobs

- Remove 1,300 acres of distressed real estate from the market

- Add 1,100 acres of small and walkable parks and increase the ratio of parks per thousand by 48 percent in disadvantaged communities

- Restore 400 acres of habitat in the Santa Monica Mountains National Recreation Area

- Create 200 acres of park space along the Los Angeles River

Discussion

The R2G-LA project does an extremely good job of demonstrating how the geodesign framework currently works in a number of landscape architecture or planning organizations. It is a complex workflow that utilizes a combination of software applications and traditional methods to solve complex landscape change efforts. Part of the reason for this complexity was the scope of the project, which worked its way from regional planning at 470 square miles to single parcels, some as small as a quarter acre. The magnitude of scope and variety of scales required the use of geodesign and design processes and tools appropriate to each scale and work stage. GIS, CAD, web-based public mapping applications, street views, 3D modeling, graphic design software, and paper and pen all had their roles to play. Geodesign relies on creativity, adaptability, and being able to identify the right tool and/or tools for each task.

To move from the abstract world of ideas to the concrete world of a single design required creating two kinds of *representation models*, those that were GIS based and analytic and those that were CAD based, dimensional, or graphically

The magnitude of scope and variety of scales required the use of geodesign and design processes and tools appropriate to each scale and work stage.

It should be noted that the boundaries between loops or steps are not hard and fast, but more like the iconic Olympic rings, forever overlapping, each learning from and informing the other as the need arises throughout the geodesign process.

illustrative. The first consisted of GIS data that came from government and private-sector sources. Its scale was regional; the data consisted of imagery, land use, hydrology, roads, topography, transportation, cadastre, demographic, and so on, covering the city of Los Angeles. This data was critical in narrowing down the area of inquiry from city to neighborhood to individual parcels, making good use of geodesign *process* and *evaluation models* that ultimately helped select the most suitable sites given a series of green field type criteria. The use of GIS was very strong throughout the assessment phase and again when it was used to calculate the cumulative benefits of all existing red fields if they were converted to green fields throughout the 126-square-mile area of need.

But once the sites had been selected (on average, about .5 acres in size), a much more traditional design process took over to produce conceptual designs (*change models*). Preliminary design work began with "bubble diagrams," which were used to identify the strength and weakness of connections between programmatic elements on each site. The bubble diagrams were part of the creative process, eventually inspiring conceptual design sketches. Again, several conceptual designs were sketched for each site before final design layouts were decided on. These were all done with paper and pen. The design team was able to work through rapid iterations of the preliminary designs, bouncing ideas off each other until they had a solid design concept worth taking through the more time-consuming digital design phase.

Conceptual site designs were completed by creating scale drawings, 3D models, and photorealistic renderings. Scale drawings captured design elements placed on the sites based upon their specific sizes and dimensions. Scale drawings also illustrated grading plans for the sites that required

complicated earth moving essential for cost estimating. The scale drawings were also used to create Google SketchUp models that facilitated the visualization of the site designs in three dimensions, allowing further design refinement. Once the models were complete, they became the foundations for more detailed renderings of each site design using a combination of SketchUp, Illustrator, and Photoshop.

It is important to note that the overall geodesign method wound through a number of development loops that worked their way across scales from coarse to fine and back again as requirements increased and different information was added to the project. The first pass was a regional inventory examination of big issues, such as real estate, park inequality, and food options, whose primary focus was on setting key goals and a handful of objectives for each goal that would guide all other work. The second pass was at the neighborhood scale, gathering more detail and narrowing the selection down to three specific neighborhoods of need. The third loop was at the site scale, the primary focus being the gathering of red field parcel site characteristics that would feed the capability and suitability analyses, thus narrowing the number of red field sites down to four. The fourth loop was site design development, which focused on detailed site analysis and development of programmatic goals and conceptual design of individual sites.

Finally, the last step took the red field findings, fine-tuned them with actual on-the-ground fieldwork, and extrapolated them up to the regional level to create scientifically sound reports on the cumulative impact of design choices (*impact models*). It should be noted that the boundaries between loops or steps are not hard and fast, but more like the iconic Olympic rings, forever overlapping, each learning from and informing the other as the need arises throughout the geodesign process.

Lessons Learned

Geodesign processes and techniques helped break down a very large and complex problem into component parts that could be easily analyzed in a variety of ways. Data collection and preparation took time and thought, but they greatly decreased the time and effort it would have taken if the project were to be done using traditional methods. In fact, without the use of GIS, the project would not have been possible given its time constraints and staffing. Here are a few examples of lessons learned during the process:

- ArcGIS modeling figured significantly in narrowing down site selection based on specific criteria (e.g., land use, demographics) and spatial analytics (e.g., proximity, size, orientation, location, accessibility).

- Simple out-of-the-box ArcGIS for Desktop tools were used to conduct the capability and suitability modeling for red to green field matching, including the creation of contours and calculation of slopes.

- Multiscale design synthesis, moving from regional to neighborhood to site and back again in an iterative fashion, helped refine, validate, and optimize design decisions based on their individual and cumulative impacts.

- GIS was used heavily during the inventory and analysis phases for regional and neighborhood scales, but less so for site scale.

- Field reconnaissance using things like Google Maps Street View performed well as a first pass in categorizing qualitative and some quantitative red field and green field criteria types, for example, sun exposure in relation to neighboring trees or buildings.

- Ground truthing and validation of existing data were essential to successful project completion as some existing data was either out of date or incomplete, and there were a number of site constraints and opportunities that would be missed if not for a site visit.

- GIS provided a repeatable, quantifiable, scientific approach to site selection that supported the extrapolation of cumulative impact to the entire study area, reinforcing and communicating the benefit of the red field to green field approach.

Geodesign is about relationships and patterns, the grand scheme of things. Whether it's a single parcel, a neighborhood, or entire city, design in geographic space using a common reference system allows designers to work on a single design while taking into account that design's interconnectedness with other systems and its contribution to the cumulative impact on the whole. In a very real way, financial systems (real estate health, debt, and loan availability) are connected to social systems (quality of life, public health, and community), which are tied to environmental systems (water, air, parks, and open space). As population and pollution rise and resource and energy scarcity grow, it will no longer make sense to design a single parcel without taking into consideration the impact on the whole, and geodesign can help.

Geodesign is about relationships and patterns, the grand scheme of things.

As population and pollution rise and resource and energy scarcity grow, it will no longer make sense to design a single parcel without taking into consideration the impact on the whole, and geodesign can help.

Key Links

606 Studio, Department of Landscape Architecture, California State Polytechnic University, Pomona
http://www.csupomona.edu/~la/mla_606.html

Community Redevelopment Agency of the City of Los Angeles
http://www.crala.org/

Los Angeles Department of City Planning, Urban Design Studio
http://urbandesignla.com/downtown_guidelines.htm

Verde Coalition
http://www.verdecoalition.org/

City Parks Alliance
http://www.cityparksalliance.org/index.php

Red Fields to Green Fields
http://rftgf.org/joomla/

Acknowledgments

Thanks to Dakotah Bertsch, Mike Boucher, Eran James, and Abby Jones, the 606 Studio design team from Department of Landscape Architecture, California State Polytechnic University, Pomona, for contributing to and reviewing this chapter. Special thanks to Karen C. Hanna, professor and primary adviser for this project, as well as Dr. Lee-Anne Milburn and Dr. Susan Mulley, Department of Landscape Architecture, California State Polytechnic University, Pomona.

Notes and References

[1] Michael G. Messner, "Olmsted's Ideals Can Help Solve Our Real Estate Mess," Redfields to Greenfields. Retrieved September 27, 2011, from http://rftgf.org/joomla/index.php?option=com_content&view=article&id=219.

[2] City Parks Alliance, "Red Fields to Green Fields Project Builds Support," press release, June 30, 2011. Retrieved September 23, 2011, from http://www.cityparksalliance.org/news-a-events/3-news/177-red-fields-to-green-fields-national-meeting.

[3] Trust for Public Land, *2010 City Park Facts* (Washington, DC: The Trust for Public Land, 2010).

[4] Paul M. Sherer, *Why America Needs More Park Space* (San Francisco: The Trust for Public Land, 2003).

[5] Stephanie Pincetl, Jennifer Wolch, John Wilson, and Travis Longcore, *Toward a Sustainable Los Angeles: A "Nature's Services" Approach* (Los Angeles: University of Southern California Center for Sustainable Cities, 2003).

[6] D. Bertsch, M. Boucher, E. James, and A. Jones, *Red Fields to Green Fields: Los Angeles* (Pomona, CA: California State Polytechnic University, June 2011), 214.

[7] Data Quick, 2011 Data. Retrieved from http://www.dataquick.com/.

[8] Redfieldstogreenfields.org, *Red Fields to Green Fields: Transforming Urban Communities—Commercial, Industrial, and Residential.* Retrieved from http://rftgf.org/PP/pdf-presentations/CityStudies/LosAngeles.pdf?ml=5&mlt=rhuk_milkyway&tmpl=component.

9

The True Cost of Growth

Today, a more balanced and *integrated approach* to flood management and land-use planning is needed—one that conserves the beneficial values provided by alluvial fans while minimizing risk.

Providing for Growth in Hazardous Areas While Preserving Natural Resources

Southern California's Mediterranean climate and varied landscape of beaches, deserts, and mountains have made it one of the most desirable places in the world to live. Topping out at over 25 million people in 2010, the region is the second most populous in the United States, and the population explosion and housing boom have pushed many developers to build in high-hazard areas atop alluvial fans.

Alluvial fans are gently sloping, fan-shaped landforms that are created by the natural deposition of eroded materials from an upland source (see figure 9.2). Up to 40 percent of Southern California's 10 counties[1] are covered by alluvial

Figure 9.1: Crescent Cove, Laguna Beach, California. (Image copyright Andy Z., 2011; used under license from Shutterstock.com)

fans,[2] which can be subject to dramatic changes caused by natural disasters.[3] From 1950 to 2007, all 10 of these counties "have been declared flood disaster areas at least three times,"[4] adding millions to the multibillion-dollar costs of disaster recovery in California.[5] That number will only rise as the number of people and structures located in areas of risk continues to increase.

Flood management has been successful at protecting life and property but has resulted in the loss of riparian and wetland habitats, worsening water quality, and decreased groundwater recharge. Increasingly, alluvial fans are being recognized for the multiple benefits they provide, including groundwater recharge, critical habitat, ecological connectivity, open space, aesthetic beauty, and recreation.[6]

Today, a more balanced and *integrated approach* to flood management and land-use planning is needed—one that conserves the beneficial values provided by alluvial fans while minimizing risk.[7] Geodesign techniques, Esri ArcGIS for Desktop, and ArcGIS for Server have proved to be the perfect fit for the development of prescreening tools to help both developers and local government officials weigh the true costs and benefits of development proposals over the near and long term.

Figure 9.2: An alluvial fan in Death Valley, California. (Image copyright Kara Jade Quan-Montgomery, 2011; used under license from Shutterstock.com)

The Creation of the Alluvial Fan Task Force

Current 2030 population growth projections for California indicate that an overwhelming majority of housing development will occur on alluvial fans, posing significant risks to people, property, and the environment.[8] Most of the long-ranging financial consequences will fall on local governments, which are often hit with the double impact of disaster recovery costs coupled with declines in tax revenue that follow major disasters. To address these multiple issues, California State Assembly Bill 2141 established the Alluvial Fan Task Force to review alluvial fan flood history, develop a model ordinance (MO) that would reduce long-term

flood damage, and create land-use guidelines for development on alluvial fans.[9]

After considerable review of decision support methods, the task force recommended a GIS-based decision support tool as the best means of implementing a new MO and a more holistic and multidisciplinary approach to sustainable development on alluvial fans. It was determined that the toolset should allow developers and counties to prescreen proposed designs based on a complex set of scientific factors, building codes, and floodway design recommendations early in preliminary and conceptual design stages. In essence, anyone would be able to freely sketch vetted programmatic elements onto a web-based mapping interface to create design alternatives, receiving instant feedback on possible hazards and risk while maximizing the ecological and cultural benefits of alluvial fans. This set of geodesign tools could even be used to create the safety element of a general plan or a local hazard mitigation plan. The tool would eventually be given the name the Alluvial Fan Land Planning Tool.

Figure 9.3: Esri's ArcGIS Explorer was used to create a 3D view of the 2005 development on Magnesia Spring Canyon alluvial fan, Rancho Mirage, California. (Courtesy of the Alluvial Fan Task Force, California Department of Water Resources Project, coordinated by the Water Resources Institute, California State University, San Bernardino)

In essence, anyone would be able to freely sketch vetted programmatic elements onto a web-based mapping interface to create design alternatives, receiving instant feedback on possible hazards and risk while maximizing the ecological and cultural benefits of alluvial fans.

Equally important is to determine whether adequate flood control structures are currently in place to protect the property.

Step 1 Identify whether proposed site is on regulated floodplain with adequate hazard protection	Step 2 Consider relative flood hazard potential	Step 3 Consider other hazards present on proposed site	Step 4 Consider beneficial resources on proposed site	Step 5 Consider capacity to address multiple objectives consistent with FloodSAFE	Step 6 Consider problem-solving economic strategies
Flood-Zone (FZ) Tools **FZ1** - FEMA Special Flood Hazard Area (SFHA) **FZ2** - Existing flood control structure certified to provide adequate protection from hazards	**Alluvial Fan (AF) Tools** **AF1** - Is the proposed site underlain by Quaternary Sediments that include Alluvial fans? **AF2** - Map the relative potential for alluvial fan flooding	**Multiple Hazard (MH) Tools** **MH1** - Active faults **MH2** - Seismic shaking **MH3** - Rockfall and landslides **MH4** - Minerals and unstable geological units **MH5** - Wildlife hazards **MH6** - Other local hazards	**Multiple Benefit (MB) Tools** **MB1** - Capacity for recharge **MB2** - Ecological value **MB3** - Mineral resources **MB4** - Cultural resources **MB5** - Current and future land uses	**Sustainability Analysis (SA) Tools** **SA1** - Examine capability of site for proposed use **SA2** - Examine suitability of site for proposed use	**Economic (ECON) Tools** **ECON1** - Multiple benefit IRWM projects **ECON2** - Cost and benefit analysis **ECON3** - Resources for operation and management **ECON4** - Transfers and purchases of development rights **ECON5** - Other funds **ECON6** - Disaster clean-up **ECON7** - Asset management

Figure 9.4: Alluvial fan prescreening tools. Steps 2, 3, and 4 involve the development of *process models* depicted by 13 GIS map layers (*representation models*) that are used to evaluate a site's suitability in step 5 (*evaluation models*). (Courtesy of the Alluvial Fan Task Force, California Department of Water Resources Project, coordinated by the Water Resources Institute, California State University, San Bernardino)

Alluvial Fan Land Planning Tool—An Integrated Approach to Sustainable Land-Use Planning and Development

The task force started the project with a series of fact-finding meetings where experts from multiple disciplines met to discuss the complex nature of alluvial fan formation, structure, and function as it relates to the natural world, the built environment, human safety, and disaster and recovery costs. The collaborative effort resulted in the clarification of key issues that would ultimately define the data and criteria that would be encapsulated in a six-step decision support narrative that would help guide the development of the envisioned Alluvial Fan Land Planning Tool (see figure 9.4). Here is a brief description of the six steps and the key map components that would be used for each:

Step 1—Identify whether the proposed site is on a regulated floodplain with adequate hazard protection

The first step in assessing the potential flood hazard of a given site in Southern California is to determine whether the site is within a Federal Emergency Management Agency (FEMA)-defined Special Flood Hazard Area (SFHA). Equally important is to determine whether adequate flood control structures are currently in place to protect the property. The Flood Zone (FZ) tools determine the following:

- FZ1: Whether a proposed site is located within an FEMA SFHA

- FZ2: The presence of existing flood control structures

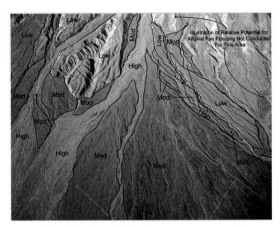

Figure 9.5: Illustration of the relative hazard potential on a geomorphically distinct series of alluvial fans dominated by streamflow processes in Riverside County, California. (Image courtesy of Jeremy Lancaster, California Geological Survey)

Step 2—Consider relative flood hazard

Flood hazards on alluvial fans are difficult to model because of the highly variable nature of alluvial fans themselves. The geology and topography of the upland watershed, the slope of the fan surface, and the uncertainty of flow paths contribute to this difficulty. Although not definitive, step 2 involves assessing the relative Alluvial Fan (AF) flood hazard:

- AF1: Identifying areas underlain by Quaternary sediments that may include alluvial fans

- AF2: Mapping the relative potential for alluvial fan flooding

During this step, alluvial fans are subdivided into surfaces with relatively low, relatively moderate, and relatively high potential for alluvial fan flooding based on a number of criteria such as flood history, age of surface material, mode of deposition, existence of stable channels, vegeta-

tion cover, and slope (figure 9.5). Each division basically forms its own hydrologic unit, which will later be used to define Land Classification Units (LCU) used in step 5.

Step 3—Consider other hazards present on the proposed site

Alluvial fans are areas of rapid geologic change. They can go through long periods of relative quiet and then be subject to dramatic changes caused by floods, debris flows, earthquakes, or fires. In this step, the analysis turns to identifying existing nonflood hazards. The Multiple Hazard (MH) tools address the following:

- MH1: Surface fault rupture

- MH2: Seismic shaking

- MH3: Landslide potential

- MH4: Naturally occurring hazardous minerals and hazardous materials

- MH5: Wildfire

- MH6: Other hazards identified by local agencies

Each MH map is derived from a set of relevant scientific criteria (*process models*) or factors that contribute to or exacerbate an event. For example, fire hazard is determined by fan orientation to Foehn winds (e.g., Santa Ana or Chinook), prevailing winds, vegetation or fuel amount, wildfire history, and percent slope.[10] Potential seismic shaking hazard is derived from percent slope, fault line proximity, the potential of liquefaction, and so on.

The current plan is to have the state California

Flood hazards on alluvial fans are difficult to model because of the highly variable nature of alluvial fans themselves.

Figure 9.6: Topography, fire adapted vegetation, and unpredictable winds fuel fires throughout the summer, denuding hillsides and increasing the chances of mud slides come winter. A P3 Orion dumps fire retardant while bulldozers cut break lines. (Photo by Esri)

Geological Survey provide a number of scientifically derived hazard map layers as ArcGIS *map services*[11] that will feed into and be utilized by the Alluvial Fan Land Planning Tool.

Step 4—Consider beneficial resources present on the proposed site

This step requires the creation of map data that depicts the locations of those aspects of alluvial fans that are considered to have beneficial values. Multiple Benefits (MB) tools include the following:

- MB1: Groundwater recharge areas

- MB2: Ecologically valuable areas

- MB3: Mineral resources

- MB4: Culturally significant zones

- MB5: Current and future uses (projected land-use change)

Just as in the defining of hazards, each beneficial value category has a number of defining criteria that are used to develop *process models*. For example, areas of high groundwater recharge potential (MB1) are typically found on young alluvial deposits that are connected to upland watershed, and ecologically valuable areas (MB2) are defined by the presence of rare species and ecosystems or important ecological processes such as hydrologic cycles or connectivity across animal populations. Examples include Sonoran Desert creosote scrubland, sand transport corridors important for sand dune maintenance, natural springs, and freshwater ponds, just to name a few.[12]

Step 5—Consider capacity to address multiple objectives consistent with FloodSAFE[13]

Sustainability Analysis (SA) provides a multicriteria-based evaluation framework[14] that allows the user to assess the capability and suitability of a given alluvial fan site for various purposes:

- SA1: Examine the capability of a site for a proposed use

- SA2: Examine the suitability of a site for a proposed use

Land capability analysis specifically focuses on determining whether a piece of land is capable of supporting a proposed land use or development, while land suitability analysis involves determining the fitness or appropriateness of the land for that proposed land use or development. Both capability and suitability analyses are examples of *evaluation models* typical of the geodesign framework. During this step, the user is prompted to define a set of *values* associated with each aspect of the landscape's capability and suitability analysis by weighting each criterion as either more or less important than another.

Figure 9.7: The desert tortoise is a species common to the alluvial fan environment. (Photo courtesy of the Redlands Institute, University of Redlands)

and insurance programs in place that handle the risks, the Southern California region may be able to minimize and balance potential costs and impact to life and property and create financially sustainable alluvial fan floodplain management systems.

The ECON tools provide methods to formulate economic strategies for sustainable development on alluvial fans that acknowledge private property rights and local cost-effectiveness. For example, one of the suggestions includes incorporating alluvial fan management objectives within an area's integrated regional water management (IRWM) Plans.

The resultant matrices or tables form the engine that allows instant feedback on the consequences of a given design's program elements as the designer or planner "sketches" designs using the Alluvial Fan Land Planning Tool. To put it another way, the valuation step described above literally creates the GIS attribute tables that define the program elements found in the drawing palette made available to the planner or designer, with which they will sketch their designs (*change models*). For example, if a user considers low residential development as appropriate development for a medium fire hazard area, a drawing tool for low residential development will be made available to the user on the desktop screen or tablet.

Step 6—Consider problem-solving economic strategies

The premise for the Economic (ECON) tools is that by being smart up front, taking a holistic and integrated approach to assessing risks and encouraging avoidance, and putting financing

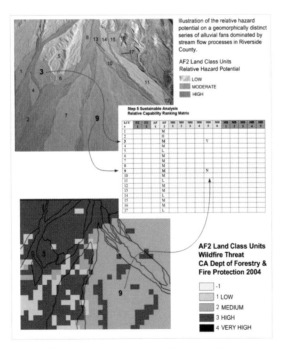

Figure 9.8: The map at top depicts Land Classification Units. The bottom map depicts fire threat. The table in the middle is formed by the union of all maps created in steps 2–4 and forms one of the templates that will drive the ranking and subsequent evaluation of sustainability criteria weighing risks and benefits between LCUs. (Courtesy of Boykin Witherspoon)

Both capability and suitability analyses are examples of *evaluation models* typical of the geodesign framework.

125

The core map layers are backed by expert opinion, historic occurrences, and vetted scientific information.

Figure 9.9: The interactive GIS map allows users to sketch various design elements directly on the map and then receive instant feedback on the potential impact of those designs on the left-hand dashboard, displayed here as risk or benefits. (Courtesy of Boykin Witherspoon)

The steps outlined above basically show what's happening behind the scenes—essentially, a framework and set of models that describe how the natural world operates and the influence it might have on the built environment, and vice versa. The core map layers are backed by expert opinion, historic occurrences, and vetted scientific information. Dozens of known design and program elements were assembled into a database that further strengthens the feedback results with sound cost estimates associated with construction or mitigation. So how does a fairly sophisticated program become accessible and easy for developers, regulators, and the public to use?

The Alluvial Fan Land Planning Tool

It starts by creating an Internet web map portal that serves various map layers in a navigable, searchable map interface (see figure 9.9). The application supports a number of Internet

Figure 9.10: The two site profiles are shown side by side for comparison. (Courtesy of Boykin Witherspoon)

Figure 9.11: The multisite profile comparison tab allows the user to select and visually compare one profile with another. (Courtesy of Boykin Witherspoon)

browsers (e.g., Microsoft Internet Explorer, Chrome, Safari, Firefox), requires no installation of special software, and runs on any mobile or desktop devices that support these browsers.

The website is secure and requires the user to log in to activate the compare and save functions. The map canvas currently covers the Southern California region and gives the user several navigation methods to choose from including pan, zoom, typing addresses, or automatically centering on a Global Positioning System (GPS) location, if available.

The mapping tool has an easy-to-use interface clearly marked with the words Start Here and allows users to select a location, review the location's profile, and then compare it to other locations. Once a location has been selected, the user is presented with a location profile or summary report that includes detailed information about the site's multiple hazards and/or multiple benefits (see figure 9.10). Alternatively, the user can save and compare a number of profiles from different areas using the map comparison view (see figure 9.11).

Step 2 allows the user to select the *program elements* or *development types*—using the icon marked DEV—he or she would like to consider for that site. These are marked with acronyms for industry-standard terms such as General Plan Zoning (GPZ), Transit Oriented Development (TOD), Low Density Residential (LDR), Local Hazard Mitigation (LHM), or Safety Element Planning (SEP), among others. Once the user has specified a development type, a drawing palette is presented specific to that development type. In this example, the user picked GPZ, so the GPZ toolset appears, with design elements including house, building, light industry, and road (figure 9.12).

The land-use suitability models use default model values to determine the potential consequences or impacts of a given development type. If desired, users can modify these values to reflect their own tolerances for hazard risk and/or preservation of beneficial areas. By simply double-clicking a drawing palette button for a specific development type, for example, road, a pop-up window opens allowing the user to adjust and save the user-defined values (see figure 9.13). The

Once a location has been selected, the user is presented with a location profile or summary report that includes detailed information about the site's multiple hazards and/or multiple benefits.

Figure 9.12: The tool and drawing palette interface. The road element is highlighted light blue, indicating that it is the active tool. (Courtesy of Boykin Witherspoon)

Figure 9.13: The land-use suitability tool allows users to add their own values regarding the importance, or weight, of each risk and/or benefit within its geographic context. (Courtesy of Boykin Witherspoon)

As the user is drawing on the map canvas, the application periodically analyzes the potential hazards and benefits associated with design elements that have been drawn.

user then selects the design element and begins to draw roads on the map canvas. The same thing can then be done with houses, and so on, until the design is complete.

As the user is drawing on the map canvas, the application periodically analyzes the potential hazards and benefits associated with design elements that have been drawn. The results of the analysis are returned to the application and displayed through a series of dials like those found on the dashboard of a car (see figure 9.14). The circular RISK dial shows a multihazard index. As the darker blue area gets smaller, the general multihazard risk for the entire design is lower. As the dark blue area increases, the multihazard risk for the entire design is greater. The red triangles on the outside of the circular dial display a single hazard ranking, for example, flood (FL), earthquake (EQ), alluvial fan (AF), and wildfire (FI). As the triangles move toward the top of the dial, they indicate a greater risk for that single hazard based

on the whole design. For example, drawing a road over a known earthquake fault causes the red triangle to move up, so if the road is redrawn well away from the fault, the red arrow would presumably move down the dial, if appropriate.

Discussion

The task force's geodesign approach to sustainable alluvial fan management aligns closely with Carl Steinitz's framework for geodesign. At the start, a task force of experts from multiple disciplines met to discuss the complex nature of alluvial fan formation, structure, and function as it relates to the natural world, the built environment, human safety, and disaster and recovery costs. The many presentations given by various experts helped define the key issues that needed to be addressed along with the criteria that would be needed to describe the *process* and *evaluation models*. The original site's prototype steps 2–6 (illustrated in figure 9.4) demonstrate the creation of a series of map layers (*representation models*) and *process models* that best describe the way the landscape currently works. Derivative map layers were created to show relative hazard potential to flood, fire, landslides, and earthquakes as well as locations of beneficial resources such as groundwater recharge and native species habitat, to name a few. These steps completed the *assessment phase* describing the condition of the landscape.

The *intervention phase* began with the gathering and vetting of best management practices for development on alluvial fans. These serve as examples of appropriate program elements or *change models*—open space, residential communities, mixed retail—that, when sketched on the landscape, return information on potential impact (*impact models*). The close coupling of design elements set in a well-described world of *process models* makes it easier to fine-tune design concepts based on existing constraints or opportunities during the design phase itself to either come up with a finished design concept or create a series of design scenarios that can be compared and shared among stakeholders before committing huge resources to finalizing a given design.

Decisions then occur at several levels (*decision models*). There are decisions made by developers as they fine-tune their designs to meet cost or hazard avoidance goals through better site selection and use of best practices. Then there are

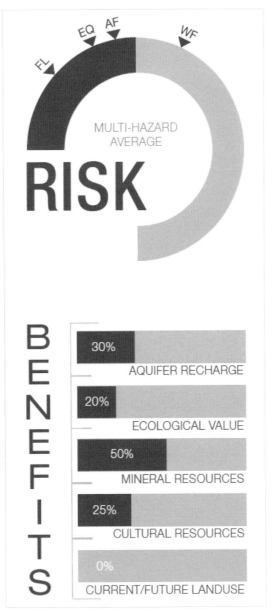

Derivative map layers were created to show relative hazard potential to flood, fire, landslides, and earthquakes as well as locations of beneficial resources such as groundwater recharge and native species habitat, to name a few.

Figure 9.14: The circular RISK dial displays the multi- and single-hazard consequences of the design sketch, while the BENEFITS bar graphs just below display the condition of beneficial values based on an analysis of the same sketch. (Courtesy of Boykin Witherspoon).

129

There are decisions made by developers as they fine-tune their designs to meet cost or hazard avoidance goals through better site selection and use of best practices.

the decisions made at the federal, state, or local government levels, where program administrators can use the tool to help evaluate the impacts of a proposed development project against infrastructure investment versus tax revenue and future recovery cost risks.

Lessons Learned

The benefits of the Alluvial Fan Land Planning Tool are many. It assists developers and regulators in consistently applying a suite of local planning tools for development on alluvial fans. The prescreening of plans helps highlight key issues for discussion and ensure completeness prior to formal submission of an Environmental Impact Report (EIR) as required under the California Environmental Quality Act (CEQA). These can both help save time and money through increased efficiency during the planning stage, reduction in the number of unforeseen design changes, and reduction in the risk of large disaster recovery expenditures in the future. The lessons learned are as follows:

- Building easy-to-use geodesign tools that incorporate existing regulatory frameworks with which all new development must comply helps ensure adoption by developers, planners, and landscape architects who require fast, effective methods for evaluating site opportunities and constraints.

- Transparency, repeatability, and consistent use across the region are vital to successful adoption by officials, developers, and the public. Creating a toolset that incorporates both science- and value-based *process, evaluation,* and *impact models* vetted by experts is essential.

- The web-based geodesign prototype demonstrates that a simple spatial decision support tool could give a large number of users with little or no GIS training the ability to select site-specific program elements or land-use options, perform analyses of alternative scenarios, and balance performance versus cost to meet their particular needs.

- Simple sketching tools allow end users to draw their own areas, apply changes, and assess consequences of those changes at a scale that is meaningful to them.

Future plans may include expanding the capability of the Alluvial Fan Land Planning Tool to aggregate land-use and best management practices and capture the cumulative impact of implementation practices across Southern California. Tying this data to spatially enabled dashboards that already track the area's ecological diversity, groundwater recharge rates, nutrient and sediment loads, water quality, projected land-use change, and disaster response and recovery could increase the effectiveness of sustainability planning throughout the region. Real-time monitoring of data, fine-tuning of models against data, and the identification and analysis of trends against baseline data could all help minimize harmful effects of landscape change throughout the basin.

Experts have begun to suggest with greater frequency that it may be more effective and less costly to locate new development outside hazard areas than attempt to control the hazard itself. Certainly the ever-increasing costs of disaster recovery and loss of water recharge support that hypothesis, especially as regulatory policies have already begun to limit the alteration of floodways when alternative methods of flood control are technically feasible.[15] Perhaps an integrated approach to sustainable development using geodesign tools like the Alluvial Fan Land Planning Tool will help make the adoption of sustainable practices for future development on alluvial fans a viable alternative.

Key Links

Alluvial Fan Task Force, Department of Water Resources, California State University, San Bernardino
http://aftf.csusb.edu/index.htm

Alluvial Fan Task Force, *The Integrated Approach for Sustainable Development on Alluvial Fans*
http://aftf.csusb.edu/documents/IA_Final_Oct2010_web.pdf

California State Assembly Bill CA 1147
http://www.water.ca.gov/floodmgmt/fpo/sgb/fcs/docs/ab1147_pamphlet_rev6.pdf

Acknowledgments

Special thanks go to Boykin Witherspoon III, California State University's Water Resource Institute, for his contributions to this chapter. Additional thanks go to the project's sponsors that include the California Department of Water and the many appointed members of the Alluvial Fan Task Force who contributed their efforts and energy to the project.

Notes and References

[1] The 10 counties of Southern California are Imperial, Kern, Los Angeles, Orange, Riverside, San Bernardino, San Diego, San Luis Obispo, Santa Barbara, and Ventura.

[2] Alluvial Fan Task Force, *The Integrated Approach for Sustainable Development on Alluvial Fans*, July 2010, 9.

[3] Ibid., 51.

[4] California Floodplain Management Task Force Final Report, Department of Water Resources, December 2002.

[5] Disaster Emergencies, Casualties, and Costs by Type, 1950–2007, table 5.1.1C of *State of California Multi-Hazard Mitigation Plan*, 2007.

[6] *State of California Multi-Hazard Mitigation Plan*, 2010, 3.

[7] Ibid., 4.

[8] Ibid., 74.

[9] Ibid., iii.

[10] Ibid., 43.

[11] Esri ArcGIS Server 9.3.1 Help. A map service is a way that maps can be published to the web using ArcGIS. The map is made in ArcMap™ and published as a map service to ArcGIS Server. Internet or intranet users can then use the map service in web applications, ArcMap, ArcGIS Explorer, and other applications. Retrieved October 19, 2011, from webhelp.esri.com /arcgisserver/9.3.1/java/index.htm publishing_a_map_service .htm.

[12] Alluvial Fan Task Force, *The Integrated Approach*, 53–57.

[13] FloodSAFE is a strategic initiative of the State of California to improve flood protection and public safety. Retrieved February 12, 2012, from http://www.water.ca.gov/floodsafe/.

[14] Multicriteria-based evaluation, a type of overlay analysis, is a technique used for comparing the importance of dissimilar things using a common set of values. In this case, certain factors like proximity to seismic faults, fire or landslide potential, and water recharge potential are classified as being more or less important than other factors so that when combined, they help inform decision making based on their importance.

[15] *State of California Multi-Hazard Mitigation Plan*, 2010, 82.

Experts have begun to suggest with greater frequency that it may be more effective and less costly to locate new development outside hazard areas than attempt to control the hazard itself.

10

Reflections on the Future

The Road Ahead

This book describes the defining characteristics of geodesign and a framework for doing geodesign and then shows examples of geodesign in practice for regional and urban planning. The case studies vary in scale and subject, technologies used, workflows, and lessons learned, but each one gives us some insight into the road ahead for geodesign.

To gather more thoughts on the road ahead, a series of questions were posed to a cross section of geodesign thought leaders working in the public, private, and academic sectors. Presented here is a small but hopefully representative sample of thought-provoking comments on geodesign and its possible future.

What Is Geodesign?

When asked what geodesign is, there was a great deal of consensus among respondents, most of whom saw geodesign as a way to do better, more efficient, more context-sensitive design and planning by connecting design to place using spatially aware tools. Interestingly, one of the common themes was that of the intention of the designer or planner to make the world a better place.

To Ken Snyder, PlaceMatters, "Geodesign is about decisions connected to place. It's about context-sensitive process, perspective, action, and implementation—nature and nurture integrated. The geodesign movement represents a broad range of professionals interested in making the world a better place with belief that location-based decision making provides a valuable framework for tackling a wide range of challenges."

Matt Ball, Vector1 Media, echoes this approach while adding collaboration as a defining element. "Geodesign promises a more informed, collaborative, and inclusive interface for place making. The geo approach to design incorporates nature's dynamics with an integrated understanding of our social fabric to better inform planning decisions that are in tune with the environment and societal goals."

Taking it a step farther, Michael Flaxman, MIT, speaks of "geodesign as the evolution of GIS to better support creative activities. Geodesign emphasizes the role of interactivity and geovisualization in helping people propose, design, and test changes. It does this by providing a digital environment which better reflects real places and feedback mechanisms which support iterative refinement. We are moving away from the blank page as the starting point of design and impact analysis as a legalistic end point. Instead, we are beginning to see design methods in which concern for the earth and attention to broader context is integral. Rather than being treated as post hoc constraints, these forces are now being embraced

Think of "geodesign as the evolution of GIS to better support creative activities. Geodesign emphasizes the role of interactivity and geovisualization in helping people propose, design, and test changes."

Michael Flaxman, MIT

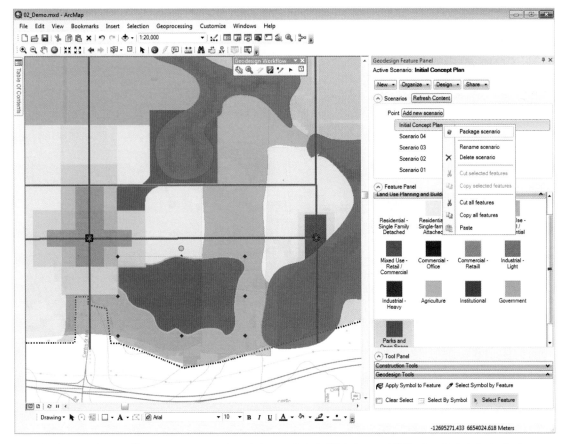

Figure 10.1: A new geodesign tool for creating, managing, and populating scenarios in ArcGIS depicts one of O2 Planning + Design's sketched land-use scenarios for the Nose Creek Watershed in Alberta. (Image courtesy of O2 Planning + Design, Inc.; map data courtesy of GeoBase)

"Geodesign is a path to a better future for our kids."

Bran Ferren, Applied Minds

as important goals and sources of creativity."

This source of creativity speaks to one of the key strengths of geodesign—the ability to challenge people to imagine, play, test assumptions, learn from mistakes, and push the boundaries of their imaginations to ultimately come up with innovative solutions to seemingly intractable problems.

Tom Fisher, University of Minnesota, describes geodesign as a way "to envision possible future scenarios based on current data" by using "the

evidence that GIS provides to generate predictive alternatives whose consequences can then be evaluated to find the best possible solution to a situation."

Taking a decidedly poignant view, Bran Ferren, Applied Minds, equated geodesign with a sustainable future, simply stating, "Geodesign is a path to a better future for our kids." As if to second the urgency of Ferren's statement, Stephen Ervin, Harvard University, adds, "Geodesign is in

the right place, at the right time: here and now."
While Ervin says he thinks that it's highly unlikely
any agreed-upon definition of geodesign will ever
emerge, one certainty will be a planet of
10 billion people. "It is for these people that we
do geodesign," he says. "It's not for the trees or
the hydrological systems or the atmosphere. It's
for the 10 billion people that are our inheritors of
what we do."[1]

> "Its for these people that we do geodesign. It's for the 10 billion people that are our inheritors of what we do."
>
> Stephen Ervin, Harvard University Graduate School of Design

The Future of Geodesign

So where will geodesign be in 5 to 10 years? The
answers varied from the very pragmatic views of
those who focused on the realities of the day—
overcoming entrenched silos, legacy software, and
institutional inertia—to the more optimistic outlook
of those who think geodesign's growth will occur
on the heels of rapidly changing technological
advances and intensifying societal and environmental need.

Dr. Michael Goodchild, University of California,
Santa Barbara, looked at it through the lens of
culture but with a nod to the hard-to-anticipate
influence of technology. "I think any effort to
bridge the gap between science and aesthetics
will take generations and will require constant
effort. On the other hand, these kinds of tools
will continue to appear, and tools do eventually
influence practice."

Goodchild and others mentioned the important
role that education will play in the future of
geodesign growth and adoption. Already, a number
of universities and colleges have started offering
classes and even degrees in geodesign. Within the
next 5 years, it is highly likely that there will be more
than one graduate degree program in geodesign.

Flaxman, an early proponent of geodesign,
acknowledges the difficulty educators will face over-

Figure 10.2: Ken Snyder, PlaceMatters. (Photo by Esri)

Figure 10.3: Michael Flaxman, MIT. (Photo by Esri)

Figure 10.4: Stephen Ervin, Harvard University. (Photo by Esri)

coming the cultural differences that separate artist from scientist but sees a bright future. He starts on a positive note: "First, I have been pleasantly surprised at the resonance this idea has had over the last 5 years. There does seem to be a significant demand for these kinds of tools and methods."

He goes on to say, "I see web and cloud computing technologies as helping greatly, so in a decade, I expect to see several core geodesign ideas embedded in standard software, likely in Software as a Service architectures." He adds, "I cannot imagine redesigning the world's cities to mitigate and adapt to climate change without geodesign tools. In the long run, it seems improbable in a world of digital tools that we will continue to separate design and geospatial analysis."

Ball and others see the recent economic downturn as an obstacle but also as a potential driver for geodesign adoption. In the near term, most cities are strapped for cash, so large-scale investment in city transformation is unlikely, but the drive to do more with less remains. As Ball puts it, "Geodesign can set a strong foundation in the next 5 years with a focus on bottom-line benefits that make the best use of available resources." Within 10 years, "the transdisciplinary approach that geodesign offers is likely to be entrenched, with encouraging outcomes for driving down our impacts on the planet."

Ball and others see the technological convergence of servers, sensors, and mobile devices as a principal driver for geodesign adoption over the coming years. "Aiding both the near-term and longer-term forecast of geodesign advancement is the increasing capability of smart mobile phones to sense and communicate details about our surroundings," says Ball. "These devices will be a critical element for gathering details before designing, [working] within the design review phase, communicating change during construction, and monitoring the design once complete." Ervin seconds that opinion, giving a clear example: "One thing is certain, augmented reality is here to stay. Most of us are today carrying cell phones that enable this technology." By just holding the phone or tablet up to our eyes, we can overlay anything we like onto our window of the world. Whether it's the nearest ". . . Starbucks or who owns this land or what's the soil type, or biodiversity—whatever it is—this combination of being able to look at these *m* dimensionals" added into the visualization of "what we think of as this free space that we inhabit is changing the way we see and understand the world as a part of this geodesign process."[2]

Snyder sees a similar vision of the future. "We are entering a new era where many of our interactions with technology will become automated and intuitive, if not invisible. Processing power and sophisticated applications will make it possible to link datasets and extrapolate information from available data, enabling new levels of analysis; 3D visualizations will become increasingly data rich. The benefits will be huge, with an ever-greater ability to look at communities as complex systems of interacting disciplines."

Matt Palavido, AECOM, also predicts a 3D future for geodesign but offers a twist to the traditional design method. "I see geodesign taking off and really moving much further into the 3D realm. The rapid advances in technology will allow the visualization and analysis at a level we don't typically see today. I think there will also be a fundamental shift in the process as well—a shift from the traditional iterative alternative testing and comparison process to a more automated predictive-type scenario where we provide our constraints, and the result will be the best outcome that meets those constraints. It is

"I cannot imagine redesigning the world's cities to mitigate and adapt to climate change without geodesign tools."

Michael Flaxman, MIT

"The rapid advances in technology will allow the visualization and analysis at a level we don't typically see today."

Matt Palavido, AECOM

The world is a complex
system of systems—hard
to understand, much less
model. Those who do
geodesign must keep ethics
and intent in mind when
defining issues and designing
models to address them.

Figure 10.5: Esri CityEngine® technology created this rendering of what a fictional development would look like in the city of Philadelphia, demonstrating the power of rule-based 3D modeling. (Data courtesy of Pictometry and City of Philadelphia, retrieved from Pennsylvania Spatial Data Access)

important to note, though, that I feel there will always be a human element involved, but I think those roles will change some."

The world is a complex system of systems—hard to understand, much less model. Those who do geodesign must keep ethics and intent in mind when defining issues and designing models to address them. Jen Sheldon, Yellowstone Ecological Research Center, reminds us again of the importance of transparency throughout the process so that we avoid the dangerous path of black box decision making. Sheldon cautions, " As technological capabilities continue to outpace human abilities to proactively understand the longer-term ramifications of system changes we are enacting, geodesign serves a critical role in transparency, especially with respect to the implicit valuation of design criteria underlying decision making." And as Doug Walker of Placeways has pointed out in the past, "The geodesign process can be as important as the tools," if not more so, requiring expert opinion, transparency, and open dialog throughout the decision-making process.

Derek Gliddon, Masdar City, adds an international perspective on the growth of geodesign, reminding us that many places in the world are in

Figure 10.6: Doug Walker, Placeways. (Photo by Esri)

Figure 10.7: Derek Gliddon, GIS Manager, Masdar, UAE. (Photo courtesy of Masdar)

different stages of development and technological capacity. "I think geodesign adoption will vary around the world. Success will be strongly correlated with the strength of national/regional geospatial infrastructures. The behavioral component of data models will be richer than today; rich data models, enhanced online connectivity, and advances in semantic web and automated interoperability will mean ever more data will be available and usable. Decisions will be better informed, but there will possibly never be a time when all important data can just be accessed. Anecdotal information, cultural associations with place, and other less tangible stakeholder perspectives will always require public consultation. Nonetheless, easy-to-access data—where all enabling technology issues have become transparent—served up in engaging, intuitive ways that allow stakeholder discourse and crowdsourced feedback may well have become an expected norm in some parts of the world."

Several respondents see the rapid advancement of technological innovation, social networks, and the sharing of both data and tools as game changers. Divisions between the design and GIS communities, planning and construction, and the professional and the public sectors will begin to break down as tools and information become more accessible. Tablets and smartphones have now made it easy to find friends, read reviews, pick a place to meet, and take the best route. Data and geospatial processing, anywhere, anytime, for any application, is the natural next step.

"In 5 years, we will see a much more fluid set of tools that will support design and planning professionals in their work," says Benton Yetman of PenBay Solutions. "In 10 years, we will see tools that completely break down the technical barrier of use, enabling the public to intuitively create and share their work. This transition in usability from the professional to the public will truly help change the way communities plan and communicate their collective futures." Walker, who spends a good deal of time evaluating the ever-changing technoscape, puts it this way: "Technology is moving so fast it's hard to see out more than about 3 or 4 years—by then, omnipresent cloud computing (geodesign anywhere on any device

"Success will be strongly correlated with the strength of national/regional geospatial infrastructures."

Derek Gliddon, Masdar

Figure 10.8: Pen tablets and other interactive devices you can see, touch, draw on, or interact with, will continue to evolve and become more intuitive and transparent. (Photo 2012, Wacom)

By combining design with analysis, geodesign can help build adaptability and resilience into our rapidly changing world.

that's handy), interactive augmented reality, and much better social geodesign tools" could likely become the norm.

So where will geodesign end up in the grand scheme of things? What will it become? Taking the seven generations view, Ferren says, "Simply stated, 100 years in the future, geodesign will be called *design*."

Where Can Geodesign Help?

Geodesign simplifies complexity by showing the interconnectedness between things, such as the relationship between urban design and health or economic vitality and open space. By combining design with analysis, geodesign can help build adaptability and resilience into our rapidly changing world.

Ball uses a topical example characteristic of the complexity that many urban planners have to deal with today. "Climate change is placing great pressures on society. The result of temperature increases include sea level rise; increased heat and drought; more potent storms; and greater impacts on cities and people, from flooding to famine. Geodesign helps factor in these pressures to both

adapt to changing conditions and build in more resilience."

"We live in a time of greatly reduced resources, as well as a period of great stress on both the natural and built environment," says Fisher. "As a result, we face a number of fracture-critical situations in which we have pushed infrastructure, ecosystems, and entire animal and human communities toward tipping points and potentially catastrophic collapses. I see geodesign as a key tool in enabling us to avoid such catastrophic events by making the consequences of our decisions, policies, and incentives evident and by showing alternatives to current trajectories."

To those working to protect and manage the world's remaining ecosystems, geodesign offers a way to balance the often competing needs of both nature and humans. Sheldon states it this way: "Geodesign provides a solution for tackling the inherent contradictions between ecological versus commercial approaches to design. Geodesign allows us to approach the urgent paradox that humans strongly desire progress and comfort but are simultaneously destroying both with breathtaking shortsightedness. Geodesign has the potential to provide a set of road maps for achieving the

Figure 10.9: Tom Fisher, University of Minnesota. (Photo by Esri)

Figure 10.10: Pronghorn antelope at sunset. (Photo courtesy of Hamilton Greenwood)

To those working to protect and manage the world's remaining ecosystems, geodesign offers a way to balance the often competing needs of both nature and humans.

best outcomes possible."

Another critical way geodesign can help is through its ability to model the cumulative impact of a design concept. As Paul Zwick points out in the book he coauthored with Margaret Carr, *Smart Land-Use Analysis*, environmental damage, traffic congestion, and loss of place are often the results of many incremental land-use changes that occur over time. Taken by themselves, they are insignificant, but taken as a whole, the impact can be extreme—the proverbial "tragedy of the commons." James Fee, WeoGeo, explains it this way: "I feel that many planners and designers never look off their project boundaries. What I mean by this is that many times, they never really look into how a design decision will affect the town, and in turn the county, the state, the region, the country, or the globe. Geodesign brings tools that scale to whatever area of interest a planner or designer needs but also go up and down scales to bring into focus the decisions planners make on those scales."

Sustainability has become a hot topic for city planning and design, but sustainability means different things to different people. Palavido points out how geodesign can help address what has been called the "triple bottom line" approach to sustainability. "I think the biggest problems that geodesign can help ameliorate are a lack of a sense of place and social equity. There is a lot of focus on the term *sustainability*, and people immediately think of carbon reduction and resource consumption. However, sustainability means a viable functional community in the social sense. The geodesign process can help ensure that communities are viable in the sense that there is equal and adequate access to services and foster community interaction."

The Way Forward

There are a number of geodesign initiatives under way in the professional communities, in academic and research institutions, and in software devel-

To create a sustainable future will require innovation on a scale and at a rate never seen before, and geodesign can help.

opment and other enabling technologies. The common goal is to move geodesign from the conceptual world and into the mainstream. Each community has its role to play in this endeavor. Think of it as a design problem.

The constraints—lack of ubiquitous, easy-to-access data; integrative workflows; and intuitive applications. Each will be addressed with the rise of network enhancements, cloud computing, and ever more powerful mobile devices. Institutional inertia and the status quo won't be able to withstand the rising tide of a new generation that will demand intuitive apps capable of answering increasingly complex spatial questions.

The opportunities—well-defined integrative workflows driving more efficient and better-informed design. Designers will need to easily include the geographic context of a site—the environment, society, and the economy—directly into the design process, weighing the cumulative impact of that design at all scales to meet increasingly stringent performance metrics. Academic institutions will need to produce ever more creative, responsible systems thinkers to meet the increasing demand for people who can solve complex problems that cross a number of disciplines. Software developers will need to develop intuitive, solutions-oriented apps capable of running on any device. And the whole intricately connected "web of things" will inform you of the air quality during your child's soccer match, or how your energy consumption compares to your neighborhood, or the "greenest" route to take to minimize your car's greenhouse gas emissions. Some of these already exist, but many more will spin off as a result of what we learn using geodesign to design, build, and monitor the cities of the future to ensure that they are livable; healthy; and, above all, sustainable.

Recently, the United Nations significantly changed its approach to climate change from that of mitigation to one of adaptation. The ramifications are enormous. Anyone who is not addressing sustainability in design or planning practice right now will be soon. The fast pace of climate change, globalization, urbanization, population growth, and resource scarcity demands it. To create a sustainable future will require innovation on a scale and at a rate never seen before, and geodesign can help.

Acknowledgments

Special thanks to those who sent in their responses, thus contributing to this chapter. They include Braden Allenby, Arizona State University; Matt Ball, Vector1 Media; Keith Besserud, Sidwell, Owings, and Merrill; Robert Cheetham, Azavea; Stephen M. Ervin, Harvard University; James Fee, WeoGeo; Bran Ferren, Applied Minds; Tom Fisher, University of Minnesota; Michael Flaxman, MIT; Derek Gliddon, Masdar City; Michael Goodchild, University of California, Santa Barbara; Karen Hanna, California State Polytechnic University, Pomona; Matt Palavido, AECOM; Jen Sheldon, Yellowstone Ecological Research Center; Diana Sinton, University of Redlands; Ken Snyder, PlaceMatters; Doug Walker, Placeways; Boykin Witherspoon, California State University, San Bernardino; Benton Yetman, PenBay Solutions; and Paul Zwick, University of Florida.

Notes and References

[1] Carla Wheeler, "Geodesign Gathers Momentum," *ArcWatch*, February 2012.

[2] Stephen Ervin, Harvard Graduate School of Design, GeoDesign Futures: Possibilities, Probabilities, Certainties, and Wildcards. Featured speaker address, GeoDesign Summit, 2012.

Epilogue

How Geodesign Will Revolutionize the Way We Design

From creating a growth strategy to increase open space and maintain rural character to optimizing a master plan to meet sustainability goals, the case studies in this book demonstrate the use of geodesign to solve specific planning issues. Geodesign tools, techniques, and processes will continue to evolve as technological advances are made, but the essential ideals will remain constant. Here is a glimpse of the potential benefits that geodesign can offer.

Keith Besserud

Associate and Studio Head, Skidmore, Owings & Merrill

Geodesign combines geospatial tools with design enabling "better informed urban design processes."

Tom Fisher

Professor and Dean, College of Design, University of Minnesota

"Geodesign has the potential of becoming a kind of *lingua franca* among disciplines and professions, enabling us to see the connections among seemingly disparate phenomena or apparently unrelated events. Just as the temporal information has become core to education and decision making, so too will geodesign make spatial information central to our understanding of the world and of ourselves."

Ken Snyder

CEO and President, PlaceMatters

Geodesign "provides a framework for communities to identify cost-effective and politically viable strategies to develop more sustainably."

Robert Cheetham

President, Azavea

Geodesign enables "greater engagement of the general public in planning processes through the implementation of interactive software and data tools that support iterative design and planning."

James Fee

Chief Evangelist, WeoGeo Inc.

"With less money being available to planning and design, dollar for dollar, geodesign returns better and quicker results, which means more value for every planning and design dollar. Who doesn't want to be able to spend more money on design?"

Michael Flaxman

Professor, Massachusetts Institute of Technology, and Partner, GeoAdaptive, LLC

"Perhaps the most important benefit of geodesign is 'smart' development, in the sense that design and planning are better informed. It is probably reasonable to expect at least 10 percent across-the-board design improvements from geodesign methods generally, with many benefits being combinatorial."

Matt Palavido

Senior GIS Specialist, Design + Planning, AECOM

"The benefits of using a geodesign approach are many. It helps to make informed decisions that are based on more than just creativity and intuition. It is a combination of quantitative and qualitative views. It makes the decision-making process more transparent and fosters dialog and communication of the decision-making process."

Doug Walker

President and Principal, Placeways, LLC

"Two of my favorite geodesign benefits are participation and openness. Geodesign invites and allows broader participation in planning decisions, which in turn leads to better decisions because no one can be expert in everything. Also, because of its interactive, testable, and discussible modeling results, it promotes openness and transparency in the modeling and decision-making process. This in turn leads to better-quality results and higher levels of trust and support from those who are affected by the design decisions being made."

Paul Zwick

Professor and Associate Dean for Research and Graduate Programs, College of Design Construction and Planning, and Director, GeoPlan Center, University of Florida

"I believe we are at an apex of critical problems that are long-term and so complex that we cannot afford quick fixes that lead us to more complex unintended consequences. Geodesign provides the opportunity for us to better understand the complexity of the solutions while vetting or visualizing alternative scenarios."

Bran Ferren

Principal and Cochairman, Applied Minds, LLC

Geodesign provides "a superior way to balance the forces of economics, planning, design, and geopolitics with the needs and desires of individuals and their communities." It supports "superior design with lower negative environmental impacts. Simply stated: 100 years in the future, geodesign will be called *design*."

Jen Sheldon

Senior Research Scientist and Vice President, Yellowstone Ecological Research Center

"Geodesign has the potential to serve as a rational integrator of the social/ecological aspects of community design. At present, political expedience drives many community design efforts. A longer view, one that integrates alternative scenarios and futures as formal components of the design process, will be a key part of a useful effort."